FAKE

HISTORY!

The Story Of How Fake Historians Treated Christopher Columbus Very Very Unfairly

A Comedic History Book

By

Dave Cowen

"I write to inform you how in thirty-three days I crossed from the Canary Islands to the Indies...and there I found many islands filled with people without number, and of them all I have taken possession...and nobody objected."
-Don Christopher Columbus

"History is like a sacred thing: it must be truthful, and wherever truth is, there God is; but despite this, there are some who write and toss off books as if they were fritters."
-Don Quixote

"I know words. I have the best words."
-Don Trump

The Chapters Of My Life And My Book

Introduction: Hello, My Name Is Christopher Columbus, And I Am The Greatest Explorer There Ever Was Or Ever Will Be

And yet, never in history has a man, who has been so great, who has done so much, for himself, and for so many people, and for the world, frankly, been treated so unfairly, for never will there be a circumstance to Trump what has happened to me, your fair narrator, the Admiral of the Ocean Sea, Don Christopher Columbus.

I am dictating this account, on May 20th, in the year 1506, from a bed of convalescence, in my humble mansion in Valladolid, to my loyal friend, my beautiful slave, and an alien to our world—

Anacabo! Fetch the latrine! Quickly! It's coming quick! Quicker, please! I can't hold it any— Too late! I've soiled myself again, these damn bowels of mine, they've been ruined by exertion and exploit, the likes of which the world has never seen, and likely never will again.

And for what? For my privileges, my reputation, my glory, for it all to be stripped away from me by the King of Spain and his feckless court of landlubbing fawners?

Many of you have heard the rumors that have been promulgated, the canards that have been disseminated, they say Christopher Columbus was just lucky, he was actually greedy and cruel, and paranoid and delusional, and a self-aggrandizing narcissist, and a shameless self-promoter, and a lying reprobate, and a barbaric monster, who was bad in bed, but that is all fake history!

Fake history, people! A fake history conceived by the enemy, the enemies of me, and of you, the enemies of the people, of all people, not just of the Europeans, or the Indians, enemies of all our species, of all humankind in fact, whom I vanquished once, and by reading this true history, you, future human, may be able to vanquish them, too, when they come again, for they will come ag—

No! I did it again, Anacabo! I pooped myself again. Bring me another pair of drawers.

I may be covered in my own feces, but Christopher Columbus is not full of poop, and he was not a bad guy, like many have said, he really wasn't, and he was not a piece of poop either, do you hear me, do you hear me when I say that, that I'm not a piece of poop, and I say it with great certainty, because if Columbus were poop, he wouldn't just be a piece of it, he'd be the biggest poop there ever was or ever will be, OK, we all clear on that, how Columbus isn't poop, but if he was, he wouldn't be just a piece, he'd be huge, he'd be the best and most important poop in history, we're clear, OK, good, let's start the book!

...

Dreams From My Father

Some say that since Columbus was born to a weaver
of medium rank and middling means in Genoa,
Italy, I was not an élite, but I grew up to meet these
people, they call themselves the élite, but they are
stone cold losers, I have much more brains and I
have much nicer boats than they do, and they say
they're the élite, I sailed across The Great Ocean,
and they didn't, I'm the super élite!

Also, my ancestors were people of high rank and
had once been wealthy, so I was regular élite, too.

My father, Domenico, a very respectable regular
élite, inspired me to be an explorer, as, besides
being a prosperous weaver, he was also a
widely-regarded tavern keeper, who kept his tavern
for the Fregoso political party, who had been in
power at the time of my birth, but whose control of
Genoa had been slipping since then.

I remember one night, when I was eight years old, the remaining Fregosos crowded into my father's tavern, as the rival Adornos, who had been rioting and assassinating my father's friends, shooting them in the back in the streets, like cowards, were growing stronger by the day, by the hour, frankly, and there was talk of departing Genoa that night, before the Adornos could overrun them.

As most of the men were set to leave the tavern in the dark of night to prepare a galley, my father jumped up, on top of his big, beautiful bar, and smashed a bottle of very expensive wine on the counter, declaring, "Silence!"

A man screamed out, in pain, as the glass had shattered into his eye.

"Sorry about that, Leonardo," my father said. "Someone attend to him, immediately. But the rest of you, listen. We can dream of leaving our city and searching for a new place to live, a new land to call home, to be free of our problems here. But where is there to go? And even if there were a new place to

go, would we not bring our problems there? Or
would we not find new, more intractable problems
there? I say: We stay here, in Genoa, our home,
where we belong, and never leave, forever!"

The Fregosos cheered and smashed more bottles of
even more expensive wine, the best in the city, and
one of the bottles cut the other eye of Leonardo, but
my father had never been more popular, but when
they all ran outside, just fifty yards, into the Porta
di Sant'Andrea, the Adornos cornered and
slaughtered them all, all but my father, who had
stayed back with me to clean up the broken glass in
the tavern, and so he was unharmed, however, he
had lost every last one of his friends and allies, and
we went from respected to despised overnight, from
regular élite to not at all, all because he believed in
staying home with what you knew, and couldn't
imagine exploring what was novel and afar.

That's because my father couldn't dream, not
literally, he did dream while sleeping, but those
dreams were provincial and not big enough, and so
I got dreams from my father's example, but not

because he taught me how to dream properly

himself, because he was a bad example, because he

was actually kind of a middling father, though I

guess he did raise a super élite son, so maybe he

wasn't so bad after all, I do miss him sometimes, as

even though he didn't want to leave Genoa, he did

teach me how to sail on Sundays, his day off, on a

little dinghy he stocked with beer and victuals, and

I have very nice memories of me and him and those

Sundays on his little boat, and so, yes, I do wonder

if he would've been proud of all I accomplished for

myself, and for the world, and I guess for him, too,

but then I usually think there's no way he wouldn't

have been proud of me, because everyone in the

history of the entire world is proud of me and will

be for all time, and he is a member of the history of

the entire world, so that must've been true, though

that's not what this book is about, my father,

because no one important who has ever lived or will

ever live has ever written or will ever write a book

about their father, or getting their dreams from

him, and I might even cut this chapter, we'll see.

...

Most People Don't Know A Lot Of Things That I Know

It's true, most people didn't know a lot of things that I knew, though one of those things wasn't that the world is round, actually, a lot of people knew that, and, in fact, most people don't realize how many people knew that.

What people didn't know was that you could sail all the way around, as they thought that it was too far, that no man could ever do it, and like my father, they couldn't find in themselves the capacity to imagine that what was impossible was actually—

Anacabo! Are you still writing this down? I can't see you. For a man with such vision, a true visionary, to go blind is as cruel as—Are you writing this down or what? Oh. OK. Thank you. Where was I? Right—

They also couldn't find Paolo dal Pozzo Toscanelli's maps of the world, which showed that it was indeed possible to sail to the grand land of the Kublai

Khan's Mongol Empire in Asia, and its gold and spices, with nothing in the way whatsoever, just the Great Ocean, which the maps showed was small enough to traverse in a few weeks, for me at least.

Also, most people don't know how I discovered the map, so I will tell you that story now, it is a great story, and it is that, after experiencing my family's failure as a result of my father's landlubbing narrow-mindedness, I resolved to make my life great again on the sea, so in May of 1476, I boarded the *Bechella* as a seaman apprentice, sailing to Portugal, but right before we could get there, an infamously smelly French pirate, Guillaume de Casenove, began stalking us off the coast.

My fellow Genoese sailors were pusillanimous pansies and wanted to try to skirt by the notoriously noxious pirate, but I told them the legend of Casenove, that he carried a big war chest of gold so full it could furnish an entire fleet, so our captain sailed our ship straight at the legendarily putrid pirate, and ordered our men to harness our boat to theirs, but the pirates hopped on board ours first, and the stench and the might of Casenove and his men overpowered my cowardly countrymen.

By the end of the day, no one had found the war chest of gold, and our ship had been sunk by the magnificently malodorous pirate, with a loss of fellow Genoese life in the hundreds, if not thousands, but I had found the famously fetid pirate's small chest of maps, which is actually more valuable than a bigger chest of gold, that's another thing most people didn't know that I did know, and they didn't know it because I didn't tell them.

So I took the maps from that illustriously stinky pirate, and I swam off by myself on a buoyant piece of shipwreck, while my fellow countrymen died and drowned all around me, there may have even have been tens of thousands of them, but I am such a good swimmer that I landed myself right on the shore of the ancient town of Lagos in Portugal, near the most westerly point of Europe, the perfect place to lead an expedition west to the East.

...

The Love Of My Life

What a country, Portugal! Am I right? It's a very important country that welcomed me right away, even though I was Italian, is that so bad?

When King João took it over in 1476, and he took it over very strongly, it became the capital of exploration with its invention of caravel ships that were the biggest and best the world had ever seen, but they are very expensive, and to receive the proper financing for them you needed to be well-connected or make a lot of money very quickly.

I tried my hand at the latter first, via the slave trade, which was very big at the time, as everyone was saying you've got to get into the slave trade, Columbus, it's big business, it's very big business, the slave trade, so I got right into it, because, you see, The Pope had just given Portugal the exclusive right to enslave the Saracens, also known as the Muslims, via an official papal bull, so it was open season in Guinea, where I imported entire Muslim slave families to Portugal by the boatload.

The Saracens, though, proved to be quite a disagreeable people, or at least disagreeable to slavery, and I had to give too many refunds when they ran away or killed themselves, instead of cooperating, and a bunch of the families even declared a Fatwa on me, but they died of starvation before they could kill me, or maybe my colleague murdered them first, I can't remember, it's not a very important period of my life.

Point is: I met my wife! Her name was Filipa Moniz, and she was a patron of The Convento dos Santos, whose nuns provided for the wives and daughters of Portuguese heroes at sea, and they had gone through about twenty of my Muslim slaves in a month, but after each one ran away or killed himself, or had run away and been caught, and then been killed or killed himself, I delivered a new one to the nuns, and Filipa was impressed by my devotion and ability to provide for the convent, and I, myself, was equally impressed by her wellborn

background and wide connections to the
Portuguese nobility, so I proposed marriage to her,
and she accepted, and we married, even though she
was incredibly ugly, in visage and in personality,
her face almost as foul as her soul, but, like I said, I
loved her standing in the exclusive world that
funded Portuguese exploration, which was the true
love of my life, and so she became my wife.

No! Not anymore, Anacabo. My wife she is not, it's
just you in my life now, I swear it!

She was terrific in bed though, my first wife Filipa,
even though she wouldn't want me to say that, but
she was, and I also never heard her fart, and I was
never aware of any of her bowel movements.

But she is not you, Anacabo! I know I have not
married you yet. But the time will come when I let
you make an honest man out of me again, you will
have your night. But, for now, can you wash my
toes? Don't be afraid of the warts!

...

My Very Good Friend King João Who Is A Big Supporter Of Me And Has Been For A Long Time

Some people called Portugal's King João "The Tyrant," because he put a rival to the throne, Fernando II, Duke of Braganza, on trial for treason and had him guillotined, and also because he personally knifed to death his cousin, another rival to the throne, Infante Diogo, Duke of Viseu, even though he was his wife's kin, and for a number of similar brutal acts of violence, but, in fact, João is a really great guy, who got along with me very well, and has said many nice things about me, and he was just protecting his throne, you always gotta watch the throne.

Living in Portugal with my well-connected wife, I had many opportunities to present my proposal for a sea route to Asia to João, and each time I requested three caravels for the expedition, food, supplies, and goods to barter with the people there, which was all pretty standard boilerplate stuff, so

João was ready to cut me the check, when we hit a
little sticking point, in that I wanted a title for
myself and my descendants, preferably "Knight of
the Golden Spurs," but I would settle for "Admiral
of the Ocean Sea," and I wanted all the privileges of
my titular rank, and monetary revenues, and legal
immunities, which came with that, and also an
official designation as "Viceroy and Governor
Forever Of All The Lands Discovered Either By Me
Or As A Result Of Me Forever" and also 1/10th of
all the money accrued to the Portuguese crown in
terms of gold, silver, bronze, diamonds, pearls,
gemstones, make that any stone that might become
valuable in the future, and, of course, the spices,
people love spices, and, just to be safe, all other
things of value of whatever sort, type, or variety,
that should be bought, traded, found, or captured
throughout the lands I discovered or had been
discovered as a result of me, which was, again,
pretty standard boilerplate stuff.

João greatly respected me, it's very widely known
how much he respected me, and as I said above, he
has said many nice things about me, and he always

will, but behind João's back, someone in his court
insidiously commissioned a secret trip to Asia
based on the knowledge I had shared only with
João, though some people who work in intelligence
said that João himself ordered the illicit expedition,
I will tell you, I questioned João, and he was
extremely strong and powerful in his denial, and I
don't see any reason why it would've been him, and,
even so, the rival, illegitimate voyage ended in ruin.

Nevertheless, this very minor sticking point
between my very good friend, João, and me had
gone on for eight years, and some have said that
during the eight years time of the sticking point,
during the prime of Columbus' life, which he would
never get back, mind you, it's a very important
time, your prime, it was said by many that
Columbus had started to turn extremely bitter
about his lack of career success, during his prime,
can you even imagine not doing what you want to
do during the prime of your life, it's very sad, and it
was said that when he started to believe he would
never get to live out his dream, it began to consume
him and turn him into an insufferable boor and

petulant brat, who only cheered up when people
pitied him enough to let him ramble on about his
vision and how no one could see it, besides him,
because his vision was so much sharper and clearer
and insightful than everyone else's, and that he was
so desperate to realize his passion project, which he
so doggedly and brazenly insisted he was entitled
to, as a straight, white male, and thus entitled to
everything he wants, it was said that he would do or
sacrifice anything to achieve his dream, including
abandoning his wife for a new country where
Columbus couldn't benefit from her wide
Portuguese connections, even if that meant the end
of their marriage, which was a sad thing, frankly,
because it was my marriage, and I don't like to fail
in anything, but it very likely had to be done, even if
it was very sad, the ending of my marriage.

But I had always just wanted to spend some time
vacationing in Spain, and it just so happened that
my wife died while I was there, or, actually, after I
left for Spain, and found a warm reception there,
and stayed for four more years, I found out that her
family had told my friends that she had been so

distraught that I had left, but that she was also so
unbelievably decent and kind, even though I
wrongly thought her personality to be so ugly like
her face, though, her face was indeed ugly, I was
right about that, no doubt, even though she was
terrific in bed, which is a strange paradox, though
probably best explained by the lack of light in our
bedroom during sex, and so they said she'd rather
tell me she was sick and had died, than insist on
making me stay unhappily married to her, when I
had no reason to come back to Portugal, because
my reception in Spain had been so warm, one of the
warmest receptions ever received by anyone who
had ever been received in Spain or ever will be, as
well as the warmest reception of anyone who had
been received in any country that has ever existed
or will exist, and so my wife was dead to me.

But the love of my life, exploration, lived on, in
Spain, it was very alive and warm and well, and for
that, I was very fortunate, and so was the world.

...

My Tremendous Deal With Spain, Nobody Could Believe How Good A Deal I Got From Them

I have enormous respect for Spain's two sovereigns,
King Ferdinand and Queen Isabella, I do, I really
do, I'm not just saying that, I'm really not just
saying that, because they funded my exploration, all
four of my expeditions, I should say, and, in fact,
many people have said that they were the biggest
fans of Columbus there ever were, and that they
understood right away what he had been trying to
do and what I would do, and that's all very true, it
is, in a way, but they are also sort of very
lightweight individuals, who needed me way more
than I needed them, and when you really think
about it, when you really think about it, they were
kind of bit players in everything that I did, and if I
were writing history books to be read in the 21st
Century, assuming everyone doesn't kill themselves
before the 21st Century, from grief over my death,
though it's unlikely I will die, because though I am
on a so-called deathbed, I feel fine, I really do, I do

want to make it clear that Ferdinand and Isabella
deserve very little, and probably actually none, of
the credit for the accomplishments of Columbus,
and, in fact, they sometimes even kept me from
winning, and doing all the great things I was trying
to do for us, ourselves, not just me, mostly for
them, themselves, frankly, and, for the people of the
world, and, of course, for history, and even though
in the diaries that have been previously published
under my name, and that I did write, I was very
flattering to them, I think it was all very obvious
that I was only paying lip service to them and that I
actually don't respect them at all.

I will say, Ferdinand and Isabella, they were tough
negotiators, and that they were very tough on, in
particular, the Muslims and the Jews, as by 1492,
via their Inquisition, they had forced the Muslims
off the Iberian Peninsula and confiscated all of the
monies of the Jews, which was a lot of monies,
though, some say that they were too tough on them,
the Muslims and the Jews, that the sovereigns went
against the ideals of their country and had become
very tribal and prejudiced, when actually the

Muslims and the Jews contributed greatly to
Spanish society, and Spain functioned better as a
sort of pot of melting food, but of people, and I will
say I think melting food in pots is very tasty,
particularly pots of cheese and meats, though the
Jews don't indulge in that, so maybe they wouldn't
be a good people to add to a mixture, also I think
Muslims don't mix those two things either, though I
wouldn't know, because I've never actually had a
conversation with one of them, I've only captured
them to be slaves, or ordered them around as my
slave, but I'm not going to pass judgment on any of
it, of how through Reconquista all the Muslims and
Jews in Spain were either killed, or converted
against their will, or were driven out of Spain,
because many people have said it was a great thing
that was done by the sovereigns, and I'm just giving
you a sense of how tough of negotiators Ferdinand
and Isabella were, so you understand just how good
a deal I got from them, which is the important part
of what I'm trying to tell you.

If you're smart, like me, you might have realized
that Ferdinand and Isabella, the pious Catholic

sovereigns they were, actually only liked being tough on people of other faiths, for example, after ridding Spain of its Muslims and Jews, they had been convinced to plan to conquer Africa and crusade to Jerusalem, but actually, they were quite soft and weak on anyone who was a Catholic, especially anyone who was a Catholic who had a plan to do something tough on anyone who wasn't a Catholic, so I came up with a plan to pitch the Pope-loving sovereigns of having me find a water route to Asia in order to turn all the people there who believed in sacrilege and heresies into Catholics.

And, in return, what did the holier-than-thou sovereigns agree to give me? Well, they granted me everything I wanted from Portugal, my title of "Viceroy and Governor Forever Of All The Lands Discovered Either By Me Or As A Result Of Me Forever," plus 1/8th of whatever might be acquired instead of 1/10th, as well, which is incredible, and had never been done before, and also I was now a Don, Don Christopher Columbus, so I had hereditary rights for my descendants, so that a

Columbus would govern the magical Asian lands I discovered forever and ever and ever, including the son I had had out of wedlock with this beautiful woman named Beatriz de Arana, who I didn't want to marry, even though I could have, if I wanted to, and she certainly wanted me to, very badly, but if I did, she might receive some of the 1/8th of whatever I would acquire for doing absolutely nothing, her, not me, I would have done a lot, except raising my son, which she would do, but she was very happy for me, as everyone was, because it was a great thing that I had accomplished, making that deal with the Spanish sovereigns, even though I had not discovered the land I said I would discover yet, the deal itself was a piece of art and a very artful deal and it is the art of that deal that will also stand the test of time as the biggest and best and most artful deal there ever was or ever will be.

...

No New World, No New World, Just Chyna!

Some people have said, and they continue to say, that Columbus didn't find a water route to Asia, they say that the lands I discovered, spoiler alert, I did discover them, in case you didn't know, but people have said that they were actually a New World thousands of miles away from Asia, and that since Columbus' artful deal with the Spanish sovereigns called for him to discover the Kublai Khan's Mongol empire that Marco Polo described two hundred years ago, that I had to lie to the sovereigns, my men, the world, and myself, in order to maintain my financial claim on the lands I found, and that I deluded myself into not accepting the truth, which was that I accidentally discovered a whole New World of which I had no knowledge when I set out on my voyage, but just happened to land there by mistake and circumstance, instead of by skill and expertise, and so I lied about it, but didn't seem like I was lying, because I made myself believe my own lies, however, that is one hundred

percent false, that is the fakest fake history that has
ever been or will ever be propagated, because, I
mean, who are you going to believe, me, the best
explorer who ever lived, who sailed to the lands, or
the jealous landlubbing haters, who never even left
Europe, and can't tell Chyna from an alien planet.

And also, if Columbus had found a New World,
wouldn't he, who everyone has said over and over is
such a shameless self-promoter, wouldn't I want to
brag that I had found something new and even
more important than even the great Marco Polo
could find, because if Marco Polo was so great,
perhaps the greatest land explorer to ever live, but
certainly not the greatest overall explorer, if he was
great enough to find Chyna via a land route,
wouldn't Columbus be even greater if he found a
whole New World instead of just a sea route to the
land Marco Polo already found, because wouldn't
the fame be more valuable than 1/8th of the profits
of finding a water route to Asia, most certainly,
because I would have many followers who would
like everything that I gave account of in my wide
social network, and that fame in my wide social

network could probably get me at least 1/6th of the profits from a New World, even without the previous 1/8th guarantee by my title, if it had been found by me, and so, we've just proven that not only is Columbus not a shameless self-promoter or a lying reprobate, but that he also did simply find a water route to Asia and not a whole New World.

Isn't that right, Anacabo? I found you in Chyna, didn't I? What? Don't you know the country I speak of? I say, Chyna, Chyna, Chyna. Right, it can also be pronounced, China or Cathay. See, she knows it.

Some people have said that no equivalent figure in the age of exploration was so confused as to his whereabouts as Columbus, however, there is no equivalent figure in the age of exploration to me, not even a comparable one, so the people who say that are actually never so confused in their sayabouts, and also people have said that they find the way that Columbus talks to be very confusing and they wished he spoke in a clearer way, they say that it feels like they are on one of his ships and the words are rocking back and forth on the open sea

up and down up and down up and down, in an even
more unbalanced way than the way he sails his
ships, making them nauseated, making their heads
spin a little, making them throw up in their mouths
a lot, and making them want to get off the boat or
stop reading what he said, it's making them so sick,
they are so sick of how I talk, but those people are
also confused in their sayabouts, and/or their
readabouts, though not as much as the first people
are confused, though I am a little confused about
which people are which right now, let me take a
second to go back and read what Anacabo wrote
down, right, right, OK, yes, see, it's definitely the
first people that are more confused in everything, I
can't believe I would even think the second people,
I must be getting a bit demented in my old age,
though probably not, I was tested by a medical
doctor and I am very fit, except for the fact that I
am on a bed of convalescence dictating this, a
so-called deathbed, some have said, though I do not
feel sick, nor do I feel tired, not one bit, but I should
get to the next part of the story, shouldn't I? And so
let me tell you how I sailed to Chyna!

...

You Sailed By Dead Reckoning? Damn Straight!

A lot of people didn't understand why someone like me, who risked his life and lost the lives of hundreds, nay thousands, nay tens of thousands, of his fellow Genoese countrymen on the *Bechella*, in order to acquire a chest of very precise maps from that fabledly gamy pirate, Casenove, why would he then disregard said maps right after leaving Spain in order to sail by dead reckoning, that is to say, the seat of my pants, my instincts, my intuition, my hunches, my guesses, and my sixth and seventh senses: my gut and my balls.

A lot of those people who didn't understand it were members of my crew, and they were very upset with me and demanded I look at my maps, after they claimed we were lost, only a few days after we had been off the coast, and out on the open sea, and so I told them, "No, I will not look at the maps, I have things totally under control, relax, I'm the best explorer there's ever been or ever will be, you think

I don't know where I am, I ought to have you drawn
and quartered, for telling me to use my maps, when
I don't want to, and don't need to, unless I want to."

In response, many of the men turned extremely ill
from anxiety and anger, and so I had our medical
doctor attend to them right away, instead of
drawing and quartering them, for I am actually also
a very nice explorer, besides also being the best
there ever was and ever will be, and it was the
doctor's care, which I had ordered that finally
inspired an end to their needless clamoring as I
pointed out that his doctoring was an apt metaphor
for my seafaring.

"They can tell you in medical school, where, exactly,
on the human body, in theory, you should put the
leeches," I said, "But it's only when you're out on
the open sea, with no medical library to consult for
thousands of miles, do you really find out how those
little suckers work."

My men appeared to nod in agreement with my
apropos analogy, except they actually nodded into

unconsciousness, and then death, the leeches not
working fast enough to cure their frailties
apparently, which I blame on the doctor for
following his medical training instead of his balls,
which he had none of.

The funny thing is, they weren't wrong, those dead
sailors of mine, my dead reckoning had been
slightly off so far, as I had had a weird serrano ham
and cheese sandwich for lunch the day we left, so
my gut was rumbling and pained and a bit off, and
the seat of my pants also had a small tear in it,
which was uncomfortable, too, and so as my
remaining men dumped the dead bodies overboard,
I used the long time it took to dump all the many
dead bodies to take a nap, which is when I then
re-consulted my maps, as was my wont as captain, I
can check my maps, if I want, I mean, I found them
and know how valuable they are, more than their
weight in gold, but you shouldn't try to make a
captain check my maps, if I don't want to, or else
you may die like my sailors did, and so I got the
Santa Maria headed back in the right direction
toward Asia with my maps, but which I knew also,

in my gut, which was feeling a lot better, in case you were wondering about it, I had a really great poop before I checked the maps, and was feeling a lot better, and I also had my pants sewn by the doctor with his surgical kit, so my seat was also in good shape again, finally, and so I knew that Asia was not very far away.

...

Those Mutinous Pinzón Brothers And The Land I Found Right Before Them

Some people have said that the captains of my other two ships, the Nina and Pinta, the lesser non-flagship ships, that were still better than every other ship in history, besides mine, the Santa Maria, people have said that the captains of those ships, the Pinzón Brothers, they thought about mutinying me before we could make it across the Great Ocean, but that is actually very untrue.

They might have thought about it, if I had been a less strong and smart leader, but I was so strong and smart that what actually happened was they didn't think about it, I made them think about it, on purpose, so that I could then prove how strong and smart I was, by landing in Asia, right before they could finish mutinying me.

It was October 11th, 1492, and we had been 33 days at sea with food supplies waning and delirium encroaching, and I had those mutinous Pinzón

Brothers right where I wanted them, or, I should
say, I had them having me right where they thought
they wanted me, that is, to be perfectly clear, I
know this is a bit confusing and sort of an
unorthodox tactic, which is why it was so brilliant,
but I had them have me teetering on the edge of a
plank, off the starboard side of the Santa Maria,
over a black sea full of razor-sharp-toothed,
foamy-open-mouthed sharks.

The Pinzón Brothers thought that once I fell off the
plank, they would be in charge of all three ships,
and would be able to sail them back to Europe,
since they were so weak-minded that they believed
the rumor I had started, which was that the reason I
had stopped using the maps on the open sea was
because I found out that the world was actually six
times larger than the maps said it was, by finally
using the nautical instruments that the Pinzón
Brothers had insisted I purchase for our voyage,
and that, since that was so, Asia was actually
thousands of miles farther west from Europe, and
we would run out of foodstuffs before we got there,
if we didn't turn back, or happen to find a random

New World, unforeseen and unknown to all,
including me, the captain, who insisted I always
knew where we were going, and it was not a New
World someplace closer, if I was lucky, in between
Europe and Chyna, and I would never admit that.

Thus, all that needed to happen for the Pinzón
Brothers "to save everyone from Columbus'
malevolent fantasies" was for me to fall into the
open mouths of the sharks and be ripped apart,
swallowed, and lost to history, but, at that exact
moment, I had actually planned to be out on the
plank in order to catch a better view of the
starboard side, so that I could point out a little wax
candle bobbing up and down, which was completely
foreign to us, proving to my men that the shores of
a glorious civilization of wax makers, gold owners,
and spice traders was nearby, which I had already
known to be the case, due to my dead reckoning.

The candle, though, was eaten by one of the
ravenous sharks before anyone other than me could
see it, but, just then, one of the members of the
Pinzón's formerly mutinous Pinta ship, Rodrigo de

Triana, spotted the shore itself, which I also let him do, though some say I didn't see it myself, but that's not so, I did see the land, I just let Rodrigo see it first, so the men didn't think I was tricking them, even though I had tricked them, and tricked them very easily, and could trick them anytime that I wanted, because I am so great, and the reason I am so great is that I am so great, which seems like a tautological trick, but it is not, some people are great but aren't aware of it and so they don't promote their greatness, or even worse, choose not to promote their greatness, which makes them very ungreat, so even if they are greater than me, which they aren't, the fact that they aren't aware of it and/or don't trumpet it with almost every breath, it makes them not as great as they could be, and so that's why I'm so great, because I keep saying it, that I'm great, do you see, how I am so great because I keep saying I am so great, I guess it is sort of a trick, and I did trick you, like I tricked my men, but the men were overjoyed to see the land, and the mutiny ended, and I was immediately forgiven and celebrated, just as I had planned all along.

...

But Just Before We Landed A Sea Dragon Attacked Me!

Some have said that sea dragons are just a myth
bandied about by hyperbolic sailors, who just want
to impress mermaid prostitutes they want to bed
without paying full fee with stories that quicken the
mermaid prostitutes' pulses and trick their brains
into falling in love with them for a brief enough
time to have relations with them at the lower price
point, and that any story of a sea dragon always
proves to be untrue, that, in fact, though there were
some different species of animals and fish and
fauna where we landed, there weren't any
completely alien ones, and also other people have
said there were no such things as mermaids, and
that even if there were mermaids, they couldn't be
prostitutes because their lower parts were that of a
fish, and so there would be nothing to have sex
with, except their mouths, which is actually also
sex, even though an explorer who had a wife who
also tried to be an explorer but failed has said that
mouth-sex isn't sex, I am better at exploring than

both of them, and I know that mouth-sex with a
mermaid is sex, and so that is another true thing
that people said was a myth, because I have had
such sex, though I didn't pay full fee or any fee
whatsoever because all mermaids love me, in fact, I
had them pay me to have sex with me, and they
actually liked doing that and said it improved their
feelings during the sex, though that was only the
case with me, and when they tried paying other
men to have sex with them, it actually made the
feelings much worse, and so some of the mermaids,
who hadn't paid to have sex with me yet, and there
were a few of those, to be sure, they told other
mermaids they didn't believe that paying any man
would ever make them enjoy sex more, when they
were supposed to be the ones getting paid for sex,
they didn't believe that was a real thing, and so they
thought that the man that did this, me, Columbus,
was a myth myself, so you can see that what is myth
and what is truth can get very mixed up very easily,
and truth is a slippery thing like a mermaid's tail,
except when I tell it, which is when it's true.

And so, like I said, there was a sea dragon, and it
was the biggest there ever was, ten times the size of
Michelangelo's David, and way more awe-inspiring
and sublime, and beautiful, frankly, the David was
just finished in 1504, for those who don't know it
and I think there will be many people in the future
who won't know it, because it will not hold up to
history another quarter century, if it doesn't get
another better chisel from a better chiseler than
Michelangelo, who is a very overrated talent and a
very unstable genius, except he's not a genius, he's
just unstable, and so we need to re-chisel the David
quick, if anyone is ever to know it and understand
my analogy properly in the future, which is very
important to me and the world, and also, I like
Raphael!

But the bigger point is: I don't know about the other
sailors' stories, as sailors say all sailors are liars,
and I would say that's true of every sailor but me,
because the sea dragon that I definitely saw, besides
swimming in the sea, with massive fins bigger than
any whale, it also had giant wings and could fly
above the water, and also besides having sharper

teeth than any shark, the sea dragon could also
breathe fire out of its mouth, and it could also shoot
ice balls out of its nose, though that may have only
come out when it was laughing at us, though it
didn't laugh at me, it was very afraid of me, and
would never dare to laugh at me, in fact, no one has
ever dared to laugh at me, and no one ever will, and
also out of its eyes came forth a beam of red light,
which one of the Pinzón Brothers called a "laser,"
but which was actually more appropriately called a
"schmaser," and I thought the Pinzón Brother
almost started to laugh at me regarding my word
for the beam of red light, when one of the
schmasers hit the brother in his mouth and shut it
right up, and the sea dragon, it could also talk, it
said, "Hark! I amth the sea dragonth who
controlleth the entraneth to this landeth, and you,
Columbuth, you musteth meth slayeth, beforeth
youth canth haveth itsth richesth!" and I couldn't
tell if the sea dragon had a lisp that got worse as he
spoke or just a pretentious affectation to add th's
onto words that didn't have th's, but that's what it
said, verbatim, did you catch all that Anacabo? Or
should I say Anacaboth? Hath!

OK, where were we, right, now, you have to remember, we had been without food and clean drinking water for many days, in fact, we had been without clean drinking water since we left, because I thought it was weighing us down, and that we would get to Asia in a faster time, a time that was faster than the time we would ultimately need the water, if we got rid of the water, so I was very tired and disoriented, like everyone, but I was not delirious like the rest, I did not dream up this sea dragon, in a fit of hallucination due to dehydration, and it was also not a delusion of grandeur that I came up with later, or just now, while dictating this story to Anacabo, in order to make my travels seem more important than they were, like many people have said about me, but who are liars, including many of the surviving members of my crew, who claimed there had been no sea dragon.

What actually happened was no one else could see the sea dragon, because the sea dragon only had beef with me, so they thought I was mad, and they wouldn't help me ready our cannons, also because

they were so weak due to the lack of water, but I
was not, because even though I love water, it needs
me more than I need it, so I had to go down below
deck, and strike the cannon myself, even though
such a task is below a man of my stature, a captain,
after all, The Admiral of the Ocean Sea, of all
people, and this should really have been done by a
lowly cannon-boy, but, all our lives were at stake,
including the derelict cannon-boy's worthless life,
so I did what any captain worth their sea-salt in
gold would do, I lit the cannon and its fifty pound
ball of steel shot out of its barrel, and, even though
the sea dragon breathed fire at the cannonball, and
even though the sea dragon shot it with its ice balls,
and even though the sea dragon also fired its
schmasers at it, the cannonball tore right through
the sea dragon's awe-inspiring, beautiful, sublime,
better-than-Michelangelo's-entire-ocuvre face, and
killed it with one blow.

Or, at least, that's what I think happened, because I
had actually been standing behind the cannon when
I fired it, which I guess you shouldn't do, because
the backfire can kill you, if you stand there, or so

46

I've been told, but then again I didn't die, so that
clearly wasn't true, and also how should I have
known that, I am not a low-class cannon-boy, I'm
the captain, I have bigger fish to fry than firing a
cannon, like big sea dragon fish that needed to be
killed, and then fried, which was some of the best
seafood I've ever eaten, and if I had had the time I
would've started a chain of restaurants called Seaya
Dragon that would've served sea dragon prepared
many ways, and maybe also with this landbird I
found in Asia as well, called turkey, sort of an Asian
surf and turf fusion, the sea dragon and the turkey,
and it would have been the best restaurant chain in
the world, serving billions of people, but I had
much more important things to think of at the time,
that is, landing and getting the gold and fame.

When I woke up, the low-born cannon-boy
informed me the sea dragon was dead, or, rather,
he said there had been no sea dragon at all, and I
had had a truly monstrous fever dream and had wet
myself, but I believe he had actually wet himself on
me, in just a specific way as to make it seem like I
had wet myself, because it seemed like he was a

cunning cannon-boy on account of the fact that he
had gotten me to do his work instead of himself
doing it, and so I threatened to not let him onto
land to get water, or anyone else onto land to get
water, who doubted the veracity of my sea dragon
story, and so they all changed their story back to my
version, and I had them drop the anchor and ready
our dinghies, in order to get some water and
explore the new land I had found and won from the
sea dragon, who had been no match for me, not that
that was a surprise or anything, and everyone went
onto the land, except for the wily cannon-boy who I
had stand behind the cannon as I fired it, this time
to announce our arrival, and, indeed, he did die, the
sly cannon-boy, due to the fact that he was standing
behind it as I fired it, so he was right about that at
least, but he wasn't right in the sense that he was
not as sly as me or as he thought he was, and died,
and now I'm feeling hungry, maybe we should take
a break and eat something, Anacabo, I wish we had
some sea dragon to fry up, wouldn't that be great.

...

One Other Thing That Happened Before We Landed Was That I Cuckolded King Ferdinand

No, I didn't sleep with Queen Isabella. She was for all intents and purposes a nun, very prude and chaste, to a fault, frankly, the kind of nun who wouldn't do anal on the side even, though she did make a pass at me once, and tried to move on me like a B, grabbing at my privates, without even asking, just kissing me, but I turned her down, and I didn't sleep with Queen Isabella, even though I could have, if I wanted to, I just didn't feel like it at the time, due to the grabbing and the kissing without asking first, which I found off-putting, and she also had a strange ticky tacky breath mint in her mouth that she put in before she misconducted herself sexually with me, and, actually, I remember now that I almost pressed charges to the royal court, but since she was the Queen I believed she was too powerful to be held accountable for her conduct, and I thought no one would believe me, too, and I thought maybe in a future time, they would have, and the leaders of those countries would lose their position if it were found out that they had misconducted themselves sexually with many people, that would be nice if that were the case, but it would probably be more likely that many people would be subject to the new and better mores of that society, which would be a good thing, but somehow the leader him or herself wouldn't be subject to the better mores, because he or she was so powerful, or the people wanted tax cuts from him or her, so they let him or her slide on the many sexual misbehaviors, because gold is big for people, it always has been and it always will be.

But Queen Isabella did have a maid of honor, a noblewoman, also from the line of Castile, who was sleeping with King Ferdinand, while he was engaged to be married to Queen Isabella, and her name was Beatriz de Bobadilla, and she was a femme fatale who left a path of destruction in her seductive wake, and also she posed for pornographic paintings, thousands of them, and all of the paintings drawn by the painters had very slight changes in the position of her body with other

men and women, which Ferdinand would then have
flashed in front of him by his servants in a specific
order that simulated Bobadilla's moving image of
sexual congress with these men and/or women.

When Queen Isabella found out about their affair
on her wedding day, after she found her maid of
honor in the church confessional with Ferdinand,
and also had found the thousands of paintings
under Ferdinand's, and now, their bed, and was
going to let them slide, if not for finding out about
Bobadilla having sex with her new husband on her
wedding day, which is a new low for a king and a
husband, so Isabella she burned the very tasteful
and inventive pornographic paintings and she had
Bobadilla banished to the island of San Sebastian in
Gomera off the coast of Africa, and ordered her to
be married to this poor guy, Hernán de Peraza, in
order to keep her away from her husband, King
Ferdinand.

However, Ferdinand continued his affair with
Bobadilla, and even ordered that she not sleep with
poor Hernán, or anyone else on the island, and

sleep only with Ferdinand when he visited, which
he did often, when he told Isabella he was off
killing Moors or converting Jews or praying to their
Catholic God in Rome, but he was actually in
Gomera sleeping with Isabella's maid of honor, his
mistress-wife, so, in a sense, Bobadilla was more
Ferdinand's wife than Isabella, and certainly he was
more her husband than poor Hernán, who, I should
also say, to add death to the insult of lack of sex,
poor Hernán was actually killed by the locals of
Gomera, the Guanches, because they didn't like his
tyrannical rule, which was that he could sleep with
anyone he wanted on the island, since he was not
having sex with his wife, which I think most people
would agree was a really bad rule, but was also
actually indirectly Ferdinand's fault, for his
tyrannical rules over Bobadilla's sex life that hurt
poor Hernán in his pride and privates.

What Ferdinand doesn't know, until now, or I
should say, until Anacabo publishes this, and
Ferdinand reads this, which he most certainly will,
even if he will never admit that he did, because
that's the kind of shade-thrower Ferdinand is, a

truly shady guy, and a very untrustworthy guy,
though you should know Ferdinand is also obsessed
with me, even though he pretends not to be, not
many people know how obsessed with me
Ferdinand is, he likes to hold my hand when I visit
him, even more than the ruler of France, so I take
great pleasure in sharing this, as Ferdinand has also
proven himself to be very mean and unfair to me, in
regards to the lands I discovered for myself, and
him, and the world, and my privileges due from
that, as I will tell you later, even though that doesn't
bother me, though people have said it does, but it
doesn't, nothing bothers me, I never complain, and
so what I'd like to tell you, the reader, and
Ferdinand, I know you are reading this right now,
hahaha, read this and weep, old buddy, is that:

On Columbus' outward voyage to Asia, he took the
liberty of swinging by Gomera for a few days in
September of 1492, ostensibly to avoid a tempest,
but actually to have a wet and wild romantic
encounter with your mistress-wife, Beatriz de
Bobadilla, three days and nights of wet and wild
sex, I should say, and she said it was the best of her

life, even better than the time in the church confessional on the day of your wedding to your wife Isabella, much better, in fact, so much better that she actually forgot that time altogether, and I had to remind her that it was better, even though she forgot again all about all of your times, after another bout of our sex-making, but no, Anacabo, they weren't the best sex sessions of my life, those have been with you, and also some of them were with Filipa, if I'm being totally honest, though, like I said, she probably wouldn't want me to say that, though Bobadilla would've wanted me to say that about her, but I am a gentleman, and a gentleman doesn't lie about his relations with women, so I should be completely clear and forthright here, and say that, I actually probably liked Isabella's sexual misconduct more than my affair with Bobadilla, and I should also say that what was actually most exciting about my affair with Bobadilla was thinking about Ferdinand finding out one day, that that was what actually put me over the top for some of the later climaxes during the second and third day of our romantic encounters, where I had started to get quite tired, and wanted to save my boundless

energies for the rest of the voyage, which was a
voyage that would tire and kill most every other
man besides me and my boundless energies, it was
the thought of him reading about my conquest of
his mistress-wife, in the future, some glorious day,
very soon, we are going to publish this very soon,
right, Anacabo, it'll be shipped to your hands very
soon, dear reader, or maybe we will invent a
technology that will allow you to read it instantly on
a device, that would be a smart invention, it would
probably kindle a great renaissance in publishing
that would allow relatively unknown and
overlooked writers to thrive and make many sales
of their work, which would be a great thing, for the
writer, and for readers, too, though I wouldn't need
that for my writing, because it's so good, and so,
yes, it was the thought of cucking Ferdinand that
kept my sail aloft, and that's the other thing that
happened before I landed that I want to tell
everyone, because it's very important that the true
history is known to all, especially you, Ferdinand.

...

55

We Landed And The Indians, They Loved Me! And Why Wouldn't They?!

Some people have said that Columbus was a racist
who thought the Indians weren't as smart or as
hardworking or as strong as the Europeans, and
that I thought that their land was a "shithole," and
that I thought they were "living in hell" before I got
there and cleaned everything up for them, but while
I probably did say those things, and I do still pretty
much believe those things, and I definitely won't
apologize for them, if I did say them, which I didn't,
but I could have, and I would have, and would still,
if I wanted to, I actually also believe that there are
many fine people on both sides.

There are many more fine people on our side
though, that's for sure, our side is probably 99%
fine people, while their side is more like 7% fine
people, though maybe less, it seemed to fluctuate
between 4% and 8% fine people on their side,
sometimes even as low as 3%, because some of their
fine people would turn out to not be fine people

after we started to demand they get us more gold, also it may have changed since I was last there, as those fine people I knew of may have died off from illness, starvation, mass suicide, or been killed by some of our not fine people, though there weren't that many of those, but there are certainly at least a few fine people on their side left, or at least I would hope that would still be the case, though you can't be 100% sure of anything in this crazy mixed-up world of ours, our world that doesn't include a New World, just the world that we know about, there was no definitely no mix-up there.

Also, I'm not a racist, I'm racial, and there is a big difference, and I know that to be the case, that there's such a big difference, because there are two separate words, for racist and racial, if there weren't such a big difference, there wouldn't be two separate words, for racist and racial, and so I will tell you the difference now, it is that racist people believe their race is better without proof, while racial people have proof.

One of the first ways I knew us Europeans were
superior to the Indians in every way is that when I
didn't know if they were peaceful or warlike, when
we dropped anchor, and we ventured to shore on
our dinghies, I greeted them by brandishing my
sword, and having my men brandish theirs, and
then the naive natives proceeded to grasp our
swords by the blades, cutting themselves through
sheer ignorance, and I saw that, though they may
have bled the same color as us, we wouldn't have
ever bled that way, because it was a stupid way to
bleed, and I am not stupid.

Also, the Indians were totally naked, they had no
knowledge of clothes or modesty, or maybe they
just couldn't afford clothes, because they were also
very poor, and, in fact, they also didn't have money,
and they didn't not have money in the way some
Europeans of the new generation say it, like, "I have
no money, seriously, it's crazy, sorry can you get
this?" when in reality their parents furnish them
with a wide, clandestine safety net or they have
credit with multinational corporations that pays for
their exorbitant lifestyle of toasted breads with

vegetables on top, until they reach the limit of their
credit and then have to ask their parents to pay off
their credit even though their parents told them
they were done with the safety net or were confused
about how they could also run up big charges of
credit while also taking a lot of money from the
safety net, what I mean is, these Indians literally
didn't possess money, because they didn't even
know what money was, they didn't even have a
word for it, which is very sad, because it was not
just that they were poor materially, but they also
had a deficiency in their minds about imagining
important things, like money, and also the nice
clothes to buy with their money as well.

And getting back to me, when I planted the royal
flag on their soil, while their hands bled on their
ground, from grasping at our swords like fools, and
I had the fleet's secretary and our comptroller
witness that I was taking possession of their land,
they just stood there, without saying anything,
without even a retort, or, I should say, one that I
could understand, for that was another way I knew
we were superior, they did not speak Spanish, or

Portuguese, or Italian, nor any language from all of Europe, in fact, it appeared that their pets were actually smarter than they were, as the first thing they gave us in a trade were these extremely colorful but kind of annoying birds called parrots, that, in between their truly terrible squawks, spoke our language back to us.

I would say, "Hello, my name is Christopher Columbus, and I am the greatest explorer there ever was or ever will be, nice to meet you," to the Indians and, though the Indians looked very confused, their birds chirped right back, "SQUAWK! Christopher Columbus! Christopher Columbus! SQUAWK! The greatest explorer there ever was! Or ever will be! SQUAWK!" in full comprehension, and that was when the Indians truly earned my respect, for never had I met a people who, even if they themselves were totally dumb and ignorant and naked, never had a people had such smart and perceptive pets, and so there must be something good about these Indians, I thought, if their pets could immediately recognize my greatness, and so I decided that we should stay on the land and befriend them.

However, it became a problem how much their pets recognized my greatness, as the birds simply wouldn't shut up about it, as over and over, the birds were ceaseless in their praise, I almost thought they were mocking me, like a sly bootlicker at a royal court, because they screamed what they were saying, but somehow also did so in a dryly sarcastic way, sort of like some of the newer people from York, England that had told me they were interested in starting a big new colony if I ever made it across the ocean, the birds they simply wouldn't stop praise-shouting, "Christopher Columbus! Christopher Columbus! SQUAWK! The greatest explorer there ever was! Or ever will be! SQUAWK! SQUAWK! SQUAWK!" as one bird would teach another, who would teach another, and so on and so forth, and soon there was a chorus of hundreds, nay thousands, double nay, I believe it to be millions of these Columbus-loving birds screeching my praises every second of every day and night, "Christopher Columbus! Christopher Columbus! SQUAWK! The greatest explorer there ever was! Or ever will be! SQUAWK! SQUAWK!

SQUAWK!" they just couldn't help themselves in their undying love of me.

And it lasted through the entire next day, and into the next night, to the point where I sometimes wished that the discerning birds were more like the rest of Europe and weren't able to immediately recognize my greatness, or that they only whispered about my greatness behind my back, which was certainly the case, and worked out much better for everyone, though I would have liked to hear it a bit more and louder from the Europeans, and also sometimes I wished then, and I'm ashamed to admit this, I sometimes in my darkest moments those first days, I wished that I had not been so great as to find this land and these people with their bird-pets that loved me so much, so that I could get a little shut-eye after such a long and important voyage, but that was just for a moment, and I'm not even sure it happened, the birds' shriek-praises disoriented me so, but then I thought of a better way to solve the problem, which was to have the Indians kill their pets to silence them so my men and I could get some well-deserved shut-eye.

When I woke up in the pools of parrot blood and
colorful parrot feathers, now that was a sight to
behold, the way the rainbow dye of the parrots'
feathers mixed with their blood, it was better than
anything Michelangelo could have ever painted,
more contemporary, certainly, I like Raphael
though, because he has said many nice things about
me, and so I finally had a really close look at the
naked Indians, and I realized that they were not
completely naked, I don't know how I missed this,
but I actually didn't miss it, because I'm telling you
right now how I noticed this, but around their necks
they wore necklaces, and you would not believe it,
though I had already known it to be true, for that
was why I came all the way here, even if I was
temporarily blinded by my migraines from my lack
of sleep from the unending praise-squawking of
those toady birds, I saw that those necklaces the
Indians wore, they were made of
GOOOOOOOOOOOOOOOOOOOOOOOOOOOOOOLD!
which was my
GOOOOOOOOOOOOOOOOOOOOOOOOOOOOOOAL!
...

The Indians Actually Weren't As Dumb As I Thought And How They Tried To Jew Me Out Of My Gold

Through the parrot situation the Indians and I had started communicating via hand motions, and I had gotten quite good at interpreting what they were motioning to me, but they were less good at interpreting what I motioned, though some said they were pretending not to understand me, or that I was actually the one who was bad at interpreting them, because I was more interested in hearing what I wanted than actually listening to what they were saying, but those people were way off themselves, because I wasn't hearing or listening to what they were saying, I was watching and interpreting what they were motioning.

When I questioned the Indians about the gold of their necklaces with my expert motioning, they motioned back that they would get me some more of it, but when they returned they only brought trifles too tedious to describe, so I demanded that

64

they take me to the source of their gold, which I was
sure was Japan, a.k.a. Cipangu, described so
gloriously by Marco Polo, though not as gloriously
as how I have described things in my book,
wouldn't you agree, Anacabo?

You haven't read Marco Polo's book?! Ha! No, don't
bother, no, it's not bad, I mean it's not amazing, I'm
glad it exists, you know what I mean, though, you
not reading it, that just shows how little people
think of him after all that I've found and done,
doesn't it, that you have never heard of Marco's
book, no, don't bother reading it, seriously, it
pleases me greatly, that you continue to have not
read it, so never read it, but where was I?

Right, I was sure Cipangu was only a short boat ride
away as the Indians only had these very
insubstantial boats that they called canoes, so for
them to get all the way to Japan to get the gold, it
must've been like us just getting around the Venice
canals, and that's basically what they motioned, but
then the Indians motioned that they had never
heard of Japan, and they also motioned that they

were not Indians, they were Taínos, and actually
that they found the name Indians very insulting as
it was similar to their word for poop, and some
people said that they motioned that maybe I should
be called an Indian, and laughed, but I think they
were laughing at how I was motioning the
translation of poop, which was very funny as I was
motioning that something was coming out of my
buttocks, and if I wasn't a great explorer I probably
could have started a movement of comedy where
people stood up and came up with jokes on the
spot, improvising them with just their wits, as I was
such a great wit, but then they motioned that I
looked quite unwell, a bit feverish, and maybe I
should relax on one of their hammocks, which were
basically extremely uncomfortable and poorly
designed beds made out of rope that appeared to
have been fashioned only to embarrass Europeans
who tried to get into them and stay aloft without
toppling over like an idiot.

Suffice it to say, I was getting very sick of their
tricks, and I was also indeed feeling a bit sick from
my travels, as I may have caught a bit of a cold

somewhere on the way to Asia or from the ice balls
from that sea dragon's nose, and so I coughed on
one of the Indians, as I again demanded to know
where their gold was, and the Indian I coughed on,
she took enormous offense, and she motioned that
we had come a long way and might carry diseases
that had not come to their island yet, and if that
were the case, she could get very sick from my
cough, so sick that she might even die, or before she
died, she might pass on my sickness to her people,
who would then die off in great numbers, which
seemed very far-fetched, and I coughed on her
again, and told her that her theory of medicine was
a load of horse manure, and I motioned to them
what horse manure was, because they motioned
that they didn't understand me, and it was another
one of my very funny gestures involving my
hindquarters, and they laughed very hard, and
motioned, are those horses there, and they
appeared to gape in awe at our horses, which we
had brought from Europe, and they claimed to have
never seen them before, even though Marco Polo
had ridden through Asia on a horse, or so he had
claimed, so they must have been lying, or Marco

was a liar, but I trust Marco more than them, because he was Italian like me, though not as great of an overall explorer like me, and suffice it to say I was growing even more sick of their tricks.

They motioned, why didn't I just relax and enjoy some of their food, and they gave me some of this substance that they called sugar, which was very tasty, and it gave me a slight rush in my head as I ate it, which momentarily abated my sickness, until I suddenly realized that they were trying to trick me again and keep me from my gold, which I so deserved, and was entitled to as a white, straight male, so I motioned no more sugar, you tricksters, and they motioned, OK, no problem, no worries, all good, man, but then they just brought out something called tobacco instead of the gold, which was a leaf that you crumpled and rolled into a paper and then lit and inhaled, and they motioned that this drug would make me feel better, even though it was slightly habit-forming, and some people said it caused lung illness later in life after much use, and, worse, it could cause you to run a bit slower, but they said it was worth it, for the little joys in life are important, and if you don't have those, what's the point in living, you know, and I motioned that the point of living was to acquire the most gold and the most fame that you could before you died, but that if tobacco were necessary to attaining all that, then sure, I would try it, but it made me cough so bad, and so much worse than when I had coughed on the Indian woman before, and I told her that she was kind of a hypocrite giving me something that made me cough on her so bad again, when she had made such a big stink about my coughing earlier, which was very rude, and then I felt a bit dizzy, and I thought they were trying to poison me, and then it hit me, these people weren't the Asians Marco Polo spoke of, they couldn't be, they must be something else, they must be Jews, hiding their gold like Jews do!

And so I motioned to the Indian-Jews, are you Jews, Indian-Jews?! And they motioned back, that they were confused by that motioning, and a few people came out of a teepee, one with a slightly hooky nose, but he just gave us a syrup made from this plant called corn, which tasted a lot like sugar,

but it seemed more artificial in some way, and this
corn syrup I soon realized from more motioning
was juice, not Jews, and it gave me a less refined
rush to the head than the sugar cane, but it was also
really good in a way, too, and I was thinking if I had
to choose between the two to sweeten all of my
beverages, I might go with the corn syrup over the
sugar, even if sugar was cheaper and healthier,
when I got a hold of my senses, and motioned very
clearly, that I was looking for the people who had
horns, and ate people's babies, and drank their
blood, and hoarded all of the world's resources, and
didn't believe in the second coming of God, and
they had no moral compass, and were also bad at
using regular compasses, because they were
physically weak and unadventurous, and maybe
should be wiped from the face of the earth, and the
Indians motioned excitedly, oh, you mean the
Caribs! Yes, we have them here, they are cannibals,
and they have all the gold, and they smell funny, we
can take you to them if you really want.

70

And I motioned, Caribs, Jews, whatever you call them, they are no match for Christopher the Christ-Bearer Columbus!

And they motioned that they disagreed, but it was my funeral, or the opposite of that, I'm not sure, because I was getting pretty tired of all the motioning, and the interpreting of the motioning, which I was so good at, I never got any of their motions interpreted improperly, not a one, and they also definitely motioned that the whole island was mine to command, by sweeping their hands toward the land, that had been one of the first things they motioned, and it also was pretty much implied in the way they moved their bodies in general, in a very subordinate way, like they would make for good slaves, which we needed, since the Muslims had proven to be so disagreeable to the institution, which was peculiar, that they responded that way, and so every one of the Indians moved in that submissive, subservient, docile, servile way that I mentioned, all of the Indians, except for the Indian woman I coughed on, I should say.

...

Indian Women, I Did Not Like Them, Or Love Her, Not In The Slightest

The Indian woman I had coughed on and had said I would be the cause of death of most of her people, from my little cold, which had actually gone away, if it had even been a cold at all, and not just a reaction to the air of the new land which wasn't as pure as our land's air, or, if it had actually been too pure, which my lungs weren't accustomed to, which was what she claimed, and so she explained that the Caribs had most of the gold and that her people let them keep it, so that the Caribs didn't kill and eat them, because the Taínos believe that gold wasn't as valuable as most people thought, she clarified that there was value to gold and to people producing material goods, which was necessary for a functioning society, but that a people needed to not only think of their economy, and that actually, what was valuable in a nation was the people themselves, not how much gold or material goods they produced, and so I told her that she was incredibly wrong, and that, in fact, as commander of this

island, I was making my first rule be that every
Indian must pay a tribute to me in gold, a hawk's
bell's worth of gold, and I had the number of
Indians counted so I could figure out exactly how
much gold per capita per year I would get from this
nation, and I promptly distributed the chintzy
hawk's bells, which I didn't even charge for, even
though the hawk's bells themselves were worth a
little less than a quarter of a hawk's bell's worth of
gold, and some of the most chinziest, way less, and
in doing so, I showed her that I also had values of
generosity like her and her people, not because I
actually had those values, I'm not weak nor am I a
fool, but I did this, because it was important to
make them think I shared some of their inane
values, so they would follow my rules, without me
having to spend some of my boundless energies
forcing them to do so, though it probably wouldn't
have taken that many of my boundless energies to
force them, because they were so much weaker than
me, and so that is how I got them to give me all
their gold in hawk's bells, which was a very great
thing that I did.

As the Indians spent their days finding and giving
me the gold, the woman I had coughed on was
really getting on my nerves, as when she saw me
writing down what was happening, so I could share
it with the sovereigns, and for posterity's sake, and
she criticized this very behavior, and she said that
people who cared about what other people thought
of them enough to write down what they believed
happened to them were the worst kind of people,
because they cared more about that than the
present moment, and I said that maybe
autobiographies are a bit self-servicing, I would
give her that, but I pointed out that there were
many great people who wrote about things other
than themselves, and that maybe I would write
something not even about me as well, maybe even
about her, what did she think about that, huh, and
she said that those people were even bigger egoists,
and that those people who wanted others to read
what they came up with in their egotistical minds in
order to feel like they had their own immortality,
these writer people were the most unsavory people,
and I told her to watch her tongue for I was
commander of this island, and I could punish her if

I wanted to, and she said, the only thing worse than
writers are dictators that some writers write about
if they believe their own lives are boring and want a
big, catchy subject, and that the people lost to
history almost always lead the most beautiful lives,
because they were concerned with leading a good
life and not trying to portray their life or the lives of
an ugly, powerful person for others to enjoy, so that
they were remembered as great themselves, too,
even though they weren't good to the people in their
regular, non-writing life, and I fell in love with her
right then and there.

Not!

The way she challenged my worldview and made
me think long and hard about my fundamental
assumptions of how I should conduct my life and
how the world should work, made me hate her so
much, and it was like we were opposite gusts of
winds in the sea, who repelled each other, into a
tremendous hurricane that sunk my heart-boat,
and was the opposite of love, whatever that is, it's
certainly not indifference, I believe it is hate, and I

had absolutely no respect for what she thought and
said, especially the being good to people in my
non-exploring or non-writing life, and I thought her
life was sad, and that was a sad thing, because she
was very beautiful and some of the things she said
stuck in my mind and kind of bounced around there
all day and night, and also for the rest of my life,
frankly, as I am still thinking about them right now,
and she said them with this honeyed voice, that was
quite special, even though I couldn't understand
what she was saying until she motioned a
translation afterward, and her motionings were
very sexy themselves, and she had a tattoo of one of
the parrots that were extinct now because of me, on
her torso, which I liked to watch move during her
movements, that is, until she started to get fatigued
from the cold I may have given her, and she started
to motion less and less, and she also developed a
cough like mine, but much worse, but that actually
made her sound even sexier, the throaty, raspy
voice reminded me of singers I had heard in gay
Paris who were not as nice sounding as hers, but
my reverie was interrupted by me processing what
she was motioning next, which was that she was

refusing to get me the gold anymore, and had even
organized a mass revolt of most of the Indians
against my rightful authority.

And this though, I'm glad to say, it went very badly
for her, because she led her revolt very ineffectively,
for what she did was she organized a mass hunger
strike, which was a stupid thing to do, a very dumb
thing to do, because that meant she stopped eating,
which at first made her thin in a very beautiful and
alluring way, and tempted me sexually, but that
soon gave way to a very scary emaciation, which I
was very repulsed by sexually, and I also felt a bit
sorry for her and the other people who followed her
and also stopped eating, and they all said they'd
stop the hunger strike if I just stopped making them
get the gold in the hawk's bells, which they said was
actually a worthless material as it would not
provide sustenance and when something serious
happened the amount of gold I had wouldn't save
me from it, and they said that I could continue to be
called commander of them if I wanted to, they just
wanted to do something else besides spending all of
their time finding gold, as the gold, they said, had

started to run out, as there was actually quite little
of it, and in fact they had been getting something
they called fool's gold for me, for a while now, and I
hadn't known the difference, which only proved
how stupid my making them get gold at the expense
of their lives and happiness really was, didn't I see
that, didn't I see that that fool's gold was also
running out, you fool, Columbus, you're a damn
fool, Columbus, some of them said, whom I
mercifully let live long enough to finish their insults
before having my men kill them, and they had said
it was near hopeless that they would be able to keep
finding the fool's gold for more than a few more
weeks, and what was their life to be if it was spent
working to accumulate fake gold, and I told them
that that's just how the world works, there's this
thing I called the free market and it means you have
to compete to get gold or what other people can be
convinced is gold, or something of value defined by
people other than yourself, to live, that is to say, to
live well, and they said that they'd rather die than
live like that.

And I started to feel a little sad, because my cold
had also started to spread to other Indians, who
were under my command, and so were in some way
my people, and maybe it was compounded by their
stupid hunger strike, which wasn't my fault, I'm not
sure, but I started to feel bad about what I was
doing, and I started to feel like maybe I should stop
making them give me gold, or maybe that living my
life in pursuit of gold and glory wasn't as important
as these people's lives, or other things, like seeing
my children, or leaving my wife Filipa, who had
been so good to me, in bed, and I started to feel a
tightness in my chest, and the world started to spin
about in my visionary vision, but then I started to
direct my pain outwards back onto the woman I
coughed on, or rather I realized her pain had been
projected onto me by her first, for clearly, I was not
the one who had a cold anymore, my body was
much stronger and had fought it off, and I also had
not stupidly gone on a pointless hunger strike,
which was causing her so much pain, and was
making me feel bad about myself, for that was not
very nice of her, and so when she died, and half the
population of the Indians on the island died from

the starvation strike that she led, I no longer felt
bad for her, or for them, for she and they deserved
what she and they got, though I did wish I had
caught her name before she died, but maybe she
preferred that I didn't catch her name, so that it
would be lost to history, which is what she always
claimed she wanted, but the fact of the matter is I
didn't feel sorry for her, and I didn't feel any
feelings for her, not one bit, and I think her name
was Felicia, bye, Felicia!

Though my priest counselor, when I confessed this
story, over a number of sessions, after I had started
having recurring nightmares of their mass graves
that kept me an insomniac for many months, and I
had started weeping randomly, and felt the
tightening in my chest I had felt just before she and
they all died, as well as the spinning about in my
visionary vision, and also I had new things, like
hives, and did I mention the weeping, I really could
not stop the weeping, and it made me dehydrated,
the loss of body water, which made me feel even
more ill, and even when it had been many months
after their deaths, and the priest had taught me that

it was OK to feel bad about what happened, that I
should live in the pain, and feel it, and come to
terms with what had happened, and my part in it,
but also let it go, as something outside of me now,
because if it wasn't me who came to Asia and
caused all of this destruction it would have been
someone else in the near future, from Europe, who
would have caused something similar, which was
definitely a lie, for no one could have done what I
did, so I decided that I didn't need to do any more
of his mumbo jumbo healing.

And I decided that I would no longer seek his
priestly therapy any longer, nor would I pay him for
services rendered, nor would I recommend him to
other people, and, in fact, I resolved that I would
tell people that he was bad at priestly therapy, even
unprompted, and that actually made me feel better,
the criticizing of him, or of anyone frankly, at the
time, the more I criticized other people, the better I
felt about myself, but especially when I criticized
him, which I did very often, as whenever I had to
talk about the mass suicide, which was a big deal,
you can imagine, it was kind of the talk of the rest

of that voyage, people just wouldn't let it go, for whatever reason, and so when it came up, I just talked about how bad the priest's therapy had been about it, that he was clearly incompetent, and his ideas and leadership only led to pain and misfortune and suffering for his followers, and that he should have lived a completely different life, and never come here, and that it's sad when people don't realize how bad they are at their jobs, because being bad at your job impacts people, especially when it's an important job on which a whole country depends, and so when people asked me why almost all the Indians killed themselves instead of just listening to me, or asked what had I done to them, was I some sort of a barbaric monster, and I pivoted and criticized the priest's therapy, that made me feel much better, and it was clear to all that I told about it, that I shouldn't feel bad for the way that I got all that gold, or the other things that my men did, which I guess I will describe now, Anacabo, get a glass of wine for me now, for it is some pretty bad stuff, too.

...

We Didn't Send Our Best People (We
Sent Criminals And Rapists)

One of the things the priest therapist did say,
during my many sessions after the mass suicide of
the Indians led by the woman I coughed on, which I
thought was helpful actually, was that even though
I was the commander of the Europeans I brought
and I was also the commander of the Indians that I
conquered, and I had demanded that title and I
fulfilled that title very well, the best it could have
been fulfilled, I also couldn't control everything that
happened in my purview, the priest counselor said
that, while he was working with me on my
perfectionism and control issues, and he had
practically said that it wasn't my fault, truly, I was
not to blame whatsoever, don't even think that, why
would you think that, for the fact that many of my
men were criminals who raped the Indians.

All I can say about that is that I hired the best
people, the best people that were available to me at

the time, and I mean, it was not easy to find people
to risk their lives to sail to Asia, when most people
believed it was impossible, again not because the
world was flat, but because it was believed to be so
far, even though it wasn't, or at least not for me,
and so a lot of times we had to hire criminals and
get them early releases from prison, which was a
tremendous procedural pain in the buttocks for one
thing and also an enormously controversial thing
for another, the pardons, because many of them
were supposed to be in prison for life, if not set to
be killed on death row for their horrendous crimes,
some of the worst crimes ever committed, and also
this prison forgiveness program wasn't even my
idea, it was the progressive Pinzón Brothers'
proposal, which they snuck past my better
judgment, because they were sneaky and they were
very progressive-minded, and that was a very bad
thing, their progressiveness, for many people were
raped because of their progressivism, because they
said that these criminals were fine, they were fine,
OK, they were misunderstood, they were good guys,
that's what they said, really snide and short like
that, that's how they talked, the Pinzón Brothers,

not me, and even when I pointed out later how bad they were, the criminals they made me pardon, they were only like, OK, I disavow them, we disavow them, even though I could tell they didn't disavow them, in the way that they said, I disavow them, we disavow them, OK, what do you want from us, the Pinzón Brothers, that's how they said it, really grossly, right, you see what I'm saying about them, and their progressivism, and at the time I trusted those brothers, they had come very highly recommended from the sovereigns, who as I mentioned before, I respected greatly, I really did, I wasn't just saying that, and also, frankly, it was a political decision more than anything, my hands were kind of tied, if I wanted the title and ships, I had to have the Pinzón Brothers as part of my staff, my cabinet of "trusted advisors," ha, what a hoot that is, but no, I never trusted them, not even from the beginning, the Pinzón Brothers, and I didn't respect the sovereigns very much either, or at all, frankly, I just needed their money, and, like I said, the Pinzón Brothers later tried to mutiny me, even though I incepted the idea of mutiny in their weak progressive brains in order to then show everyone

how powerful I was by stopping them just in the
nick of time, they still tried to mutiny me, with the
criminals that they convinced me to pardon and
hire, and I've often been told that the buck
should've stopped with me, the Admiral of the
Ocean Sea, but I would say, in my defense, though I
don't think one is necessary, and I've been told by
many other people that this whole thing isn't such a
big deal, it happened with the Romans and the
Greeks, the raping, and also a lot of pillaging, and
also in Asia with the Mongols, who were the people
I discovered themselves, the people that my men
later raped and pillaged themselves, and so, you
see, it's a circular thing, and it will happen again,
with other great countries, in the future, even ones
that think they are perfect exemplars of good
government and behavior, I'm sure of it, and so the
point is: the buck that everyone always talks about,
it was taken up on land, before we left, by the
progressive Pinzón Brothers, and not on the ocean
sea, and it was thus outside of my jurisdiction, as
Admiral of the Ocean Sea, and so it was definitely
not my fault how it didn't stop, the raping buck.

One thing I should also say is that though many of
the people who immigrated with me were very bad
and should never have been let into this country, I
did pardon them again, my men, the criminals and
the rapists, as I had hope that maybe they'd have
children who weren't criminals and rapists, and
maybe we'd just forget their forebears, and think of
the descendants in the new land as a great people,
so great a people that we'd just think of them as the
people of the land, and we would then protect those
people from any other bad people that might try to
get into the land, because we would have learned
our lesson about letting in criminals and rapists,
which is that you can't do that, you need to do
anything you can to not let them in, because I saw
what they did, it was not good, so I would break any
laws of the land, definitely any progressive ones, in
order to stop that, and that's how I would run a
country of the good descendants of the criminals
and rapists, and I would call it: The United People
of Columbus.

...

How I Started To Build The United People Of Columbus

People have told stories about how and why I started to build a colony on the land I found, the version that seems to be getting the most traction also happens to be the most fake, which is no surprise, if you're a fan of me and this book, you're used to the lies I've had to fight all my life, and will continue to fight, in death, via this book, though I will very likely not die, because I am not tired in the slightest, and so the fake history that has been spread was that Columbus was depressed about the raping of the Indians by his men, and the dead Indians from their starvation strike, and the loss of the woman he coughed on but whom he didn't have any feelings for, and so he purposefully, on a routine errand to a neighboring island, steered his flagship, the Santa Maria, into the coast, crashing it, in a fit of mad despair, because he had felt so bad about the impact he was causing on the Indians, whom he commanded, that he crashed the boat into the coast, on purpose, and made it impossible for it

ever to be steered again back to Spain, leaving them
with only two smaller boats, which were quite
unlikely to make it back to Spain alone, thus saving
the other Indians from being found out about, and
the whole continent, frankly, for it was near
impossible that someone would come along from
Europe and also sail there, it was the kind of thing
that only Columbus could have done, with his sui
generis, not due to the better ship technology that
had been invented while he was coming of age, and
it's likely that Europe wouldn't have found a water
route to Asia for another many hundreds of years, if
ever, and most likely never, and so if Columbus had
crashed his flagship on purpose it would have
actually been a very brave and noble act of
self-sacrifice, to save the Indians from Europeans
like him, if it were true, which it wasn't, not at all.

See, what actually happened was that it was this
idiot, Juan de La Cosa, the ship's master, who I had
let take a little joy ride for his birthday, and because
he had cut back on his raping, he had been one of
the worst rapists, and I wanted to reward that kind
of behavior, the less raping, even if I wasn't going to

punish the opposite, the earlier raping, and instead
I gave out more pardons, and so the creepy
nincompoop, he got drunk, the lecherous lushy lug
he was, he also somehow had never learned how to
drink and steer, because he was a real lightweight
on top of it all, and so he fell asleep at the wheel and
did the crashing of my perfect Santa Maria, for
which I was very mad at him, and I wanted to let
the Indians rape him for it, but they said they
weren't into vengeance like that, an ass for an ass is
not their thing, I guess, even with a guaranteed
pardon from me, so they didn't take me up on it.

But the other thing that is true is that I wanted to
start my United People of Columbus, it had been
something I was planning all along, it was part of
my grand plan and step two of my squad goals for
me and myself, which was all that was in my squad,
and so I did take the opportunity to use the
wreckage as wood for my colony's first fort, which I
was sure would soon turn into the biggest city in all
of Europe or Asia or any land in the world that
there would ever be, after some more trips to get
more people over there, because I planned to

continue to rule the land and the Indians, and have my children, who I hadn't seen in years, rule them as well, because I didn't feel conflicted about what I had achieved, the Indians had not been wronged by me, just my men, and in fact they had been greatly helped by me and if anything, they were pretty ungrateful of all that I had done for them, such as make them stronger through natural competition with us, as well as my creation of the artform of improvised jokes with my motioning, which was getting funnier by the day, I wish I could do it for all of you who are reading, but you'll just have to trust me that I'm a very funny person, one of the funniest in history, even if this story itself has been a very sober account, and while I wouldn't take back a word I said, I might go back and punch it up, this story, we'll see if there's enough time before I die, which there probably will be, because I will probably live a lot longer and get off my so-called deathbed soon, I'm sure of it, right, Anacabo, can you move my legs though real quick, I seem to be losing feeling in my extremities, is that bad, is that bad? Oh, that's much better, thank you, Anacabo.

OK, so after I had my men build the fort from the wreckage, I then told the men from my Santa Maria that they had to stay there, while we set sail with all the gold and went back to Spain, and they had to promise to stay there and be better to the Indians than they had been, until we got back, and I would know if they hadn't been better to the Indians, because an Admiral knows those types of things, you can't fool an Admiral, well, some Admirals can be fooled, but not the Admiral of the Ocean Sea, that's for sure, but many of them complained, they said, how on Earth would I find them again, did I even know where we were, they said that I sailed around like a crazy person using only my dead reckoning, and that only God knew where we really were, if there even was a God, which they were unsure about now, because what God would put someone like me in charge, only a God who didn't care about people, or who was actually a Child God that had a universe of us made for Him by the old God and the new, Child God was playing with us in His game in a very immature way and wanted to see what would happen if the worst people in His game were put in charge of the rest, and the real God was

letting the Child God do this, so the Child God
would learn, which is why there are bad things in
the world, there must be a reason why there are bad
things in the world, right, and also was I screwing
them out of their gold, how come me and the other
sailors who happened not to be on the Santa Maria,
why were we the lucky ones going back to get to
decide how to spend their hard-earned gold, and
see their families again, or some mermaid
prostitutes, whatever they were into lifestyle-wise.

But I told them not to worry, for I had made a deal
with a local cacique, that is, a leader of the Indians
who was still alive after all the raping and
indiscriminate influenza death and the starvation
strike led by his daughter whom I coughed on,
whom I didn't love one bit, and he promised to
watch out for my men and feed them while I went
back to Spain and then gathered more men,
probably not the same men who got to go the first
time would go back, because who in their right
mind would sign up to do this again, except for
someone as in their right mind as me, and also I
probably had to raise funds and get new ships made

for another trip back, which would take at least one
to three years they said, but the thing is this cacique
he seemed very trustworthy, he was one of the few
fine people on the other side that I talked about
before, and he promised me he was not a Carib or a
Jew, and I had a good feeling about him, and I still
do, even after I returned on my second voyage,
spoiler alert, I did find my way back, and it was very
easy, a very easy thing for me, at least, and all my
men were dead and strewn about unburied, very
disgustingly and disrespectfully, and the cacique
had lied to me about what had happened to them,
and said he had not been involved in killing any of
them, even though he had been involved in the
killing of most of them, and I liked him even still,
because he reminded me, I guess, of my good
friend, King João, not only because the cacique also
said many nice things about me to my face, which
he did, some of them even nicer than the things
that João has said about me, but because he was a
similar type of leader to João and also, to me, I
believed, a real autocratic, despotic, strongman,
tyrant-type, and, I think, to be frank, more than
loyalty to my own countrymen, or to any adopted

country's men, or to any laws, or definitely to any
sort of inherent human rights that we all share as a
species, it is kinship with those kinds of leaders,
those special few, which were actually quite similar
to the mafia types in my native Italy now that I
think about it, but it was being like them that was
going to best serve me and the world in the future,
because their way is the way of the real world, and
how things get done, and good or bad, it is the
getting of things done, and the getting of them done
very strongly, that is so important and will stand
the test of time, no matter the human costs, or the
complaints of weak people, but I could be wrong,
though I'm sure I'm not, which is what makes me so
right and strong, and if someone were to rule The
United People of Columbus besides me or my
descendants, I would want it to be one of these
autocratic, despotic, strongman, tyrant-types,
though I doubt my descendants will not rule The
United People of Columbus for as long as there are
Columbus descendants, which will be forever.

...

The Hero's Return

It's hard to express how big a turnout there was for me upon my return back to Spain, some have said that my rival Bartolomeu Dias had a grander return from his trip to the Cape of Good Hope at the bottom of Africa when he came back to Portugal, which he did first, but which was a much lesser accomplishment, and very likely rigged, they said his turnout was very large and all of the town criers and all the best entertainers came out to celebrate him, because he was very charming and a great orator, and he was younger and more attractive than Columbus, and he was more well-liked in general due to his better education and sense of humor and honor, and would be better remembered by historians, but the thing is Dias was born in Africa, he was, and so he shouldn't have been allowed to explore there, because he already knew where it and the Cape were, so he didn't really discover it, and people also said that the great plaza where people gathered was completely filled up for Dias' return, way more than when I came back to

Spain and its plaza, but actually my arrival was
greeted with much more fanfare and crowds, and
some said my speech was very poor and scattered
and unprepared and sort of crazy, and another
explorer who had been in attendance who was
much less popular than Dias, who explored
wherever he explored before Dias, who most of the
people of the world believed was the poorest
speaking explorer and worst explorer in
generations, but after I came around, they said I
was much much much worse and he was fine, in
retrospect, that explorer, they would be happy if he
was still exploring, he could explore forever if it
were him versus me, his name was Shrub or
something or other, I forget, he said I had said
some pretty weird stuff, but that wasn't true
whatsoever, but yes, the rain and lightning and bad
weather would have led to less crowds for anyone
else, except for me, because it was actually the
largest crowd there had ever been in the history of
the world for anything, not just the return of
explorers, except for my other later returns, which
kept getting bigger and setting new records, and my
town criers secretary made sure everyone knew.

Though maybe I was pretty surprised that I had
won all that gold and glory and had made it back to
Europe to the plaza to address the people after all I
had been through, and so maybe I did say some
weird stuff about carnage, because there had been a
lot of carnage in Asia, as I told you about before,
with the raping and everything else, but, you know,
no one thought I could do it, the town criers, they
all said, Columbus will never make it to Asia and
back, never, it's impossible, and, you know, the
town criers, they're very sick people, very sick, and
cruel, and unhappy, the town criers, probably from
all their crying, and you wouldn't believe the
thoughts they have inside their unhappy heads, it
must make them ill all the time to carry around
their sick thoughts with them, and they think
they're never wrong, the town criers, but the town
criers were very wrong, and you all were wrong for
believing them, if you did believe them, though you
probably didn't, because you're probably a smart
person, if you're reading this book, congratulations
by the way for buying it, and for supporting me and
believing in me, but if you didn't support me before

you bought and read this book, then you should feel
a little bad, because you should have, because I am
a very great explorer, the best there ever was or ever
will be, and same with writing, too, and it should
have been clear to anyone from the moment I was
born, even if you didn't know me when I was born,
you should have felt that a greatness entered the
world that would change it forever, because even if
someone were to one day travel to the moon, it
wouldn't be as important of an exploration as mine,
and, in fact, I might still go to the moon, as I am
feeling much better on this so-called deathbed, it is
not, it is not my deathbed, and there is much more
of my story to come, I'm sure of it, I'm really just
getting started, as I feel great, the best I've ever felt,
and I have felt very good in the past, how I've felt
before, I've felt better than anyone ever has felt
before, so if how I feel right now is better than that,
it is a good sign for my life expectancy, and
humanity's chance of reaching the moon, since it
depends on me.

That reminds me, some have said that Columbus is
a bit mentally ill, they have said that he has huge

mood swings where he is very expansive and
talkative and stays up all night and day and writes
everything down that he thinks and says, or has it
written down for him, and he thinks it is all quite
brilliant, even when he doesn't read it over after he
says it, or before he has it published, when really it
is the ramblings of a madman, but Columbus is
actually always sound of mind, and he is a very sane
individual who actually has the opposite of mental
illness, his mind is very balanced, the most compos
mentis and also the most stable in history, though it
is not slow or confined in a box, or without the
spark of creativity that is so important in life, for if
he were without that, that would be very bad, then
people would not find Columbus as amusing as he
usually is, as he always is, rather, for I am never not
amusing, and if he were to not have had confidence,
he would not have done the great things that he has
done and always will do, and thus the world would
not be as great as it has become because of him, and
so, where was I, my mind is racing a bit, I just get so
worked up about the aspersions about my mental
health, it's very upsetting, the aspersions, the
aspersions are very cruel, even though they are very

ineffective, because they do not impact my mental
fitness at all, because my mental fitness is so strong,
my doctor said I have the strongest mental fitness
of anyone that has ever been Admiral of the Ocean
Sea, not that there has been any other or ever will
be any other, besides my sons, as I will pass down
that title, and they will also not have any mental
fitness problems passed down by me, because my
apples are so good, so nothing to worry about there,
seriously, though, what was I talking about, my
mind is really racing, woooooooooowowoooowza!

Oh, right, so as I pulled our boats into the dock, I
threw gold to the people in the crowd, and
Ferdinand and Isabella clapped, and some people
said they bowed to me, actually, which would have
been the first time the King and Queen bowed to a
citizen, in history, though I didn't see it personally,
but I wouldn't have been surprised if it had
happened, because what I had done was more
important than anything they had ever done or
what any king or queen would ever do, and I yelled:

I'M THE BEST EXPLORER THERE EVER WAS
AND EVER WILL BE!

And everyone agreed, if it's possible for that word
to even express how much they agreed with me, the
word agreed, I doubt it, if there were a word to
show how much they agreed with me, I would
probably need to come up with it myself, so I will,
right now, it is that they columbused me, that is the
word, "columbused," it is from now on to be defined
as everyone loved and agreed with and appreciated
someone, that is me, more than their own life and
anyone else's life that they knew, and life itself, and
so they columbused me.

And then they columbused me again by giving me
another trip.

...

The Second Trip Was Even Better Than The First, Despite My Brother Bartholomew, Who Made Everyone Not Like Me As Much As They Used To, Though They Still Loved Me

Some have said that the second trip was not as smooth or didn't go as well as the first one, they said it was actually much worse, in fact, that I hastily assembled it, and took way too many men and ships back to Asia, and that when I got there, I completely lost control over my men, way worse than during the first trip, to the point that there was a mutiny, and it was a mutiny that I didn't incept into others' minds in order to then show them my power after I stopped it, it was just a regular mutiny that happened because people were upset with Columbus and were also outside of my control, which they said had become limited by my older age, and my overreaching ambition, and the thing about that though, is that it was actually all my younger brother Bartholomew's fault.

I didn't even want to take him with me on the second voyage, as no one really liked my brother, certainly not me, as he was not as charismatic as me, and he was a real serious type, never any fun, and people didn't respect him, because he wasn't as cool as me, and he didn't get the girls I did or play on the good sports teams like me, or post paintings in our social communities that got a lot of likes like me, and he never would be as cool as me, no matter how long he lived, or if there were a way to live again, in a million iterations of our brotherhood, maybe in one of them, he would have been close to as cool as me, but probably not, but if your brother begs you to be part of your second voyage, and I mean he really begged me, he was on his hands and knees, it was pathetic really, the kind of begging he was doing, to come on the second voyage, it was sad, I had never seen begging like that before, and, frankly, it scared me, the begging, because we share ancestors, and for my blood to share blood with him, and for him to be begging me in the way he was begging me, it made me think that there might be some uncool blood in my own blood in my body, and so instead of considering that to be the case, because it really creeped me out, thinking about my body's blood like that, I just relented to his pathetic begging and invited him to come on the voyage, as long as he promised not to mess it up.

But of course he did, my brother messed it up, and he messed it up very badly, for me, and for history, and that's something he's going to have to live with for the rest of his life, though I'm not sure if he's still alive, because I don't talk to him anymore after what happened, as well, if he is still alive, he has to continue to live with the fact that he's still so uncool, even more uncool for having messed up my second trip, or maybe it was my third trip, I don't know, the second and the third trip get a little blurry, the point is he messed up the trip that I'm talking about right now, if not both of them somehow, and how he did it was that I put him in charge of the new colony that I founded, while I went looking for the mainland of Asia, and he was so uncool and such a loser and so completely not respected by everyone that ever met him, that people tried to mutiny him, namely, Francisco Roldán, who, I have to admit was a lot cooler than

my brother, and I sometimes wished he had been
my brother instead of Bartholomew, because
Roldán had this bad boy attitude, he just didn't give
AF, like no Fs at all, which you just have to respect,
especially compared to my brother who gave way
too many Fs, like there wasn't an F my brother
wouldn't give, which was very sad and uncool and
just lame AF, and so even though I abandoned my
trip to find the mainland of Asia in order to quell
the rebellion, and put Bartholomew back in charge,
I sort of wished Roldán had just killed my brother,
and taken over the colony without me knowing, so I
could have continued blissfully unaware and found
the mainland of Asia, which had eluded me so far,
but, no, I had to go back to the island to help my
brother, because he was my younger brother, and
you're supposed to do stuff like that for younger
siblings, and for your family in general, I guess.

But when you think about it, not only did my
brother mess me up by getting everyone to mutiny
but he also cost me the opportunity to find the
mainland of Asia, and so what happened from there
was that people started to doubt that what I had

found was Asia, and they started to say it was a
different land, a New World, and some people said I
should be embarrassed about calling myself the
discoverer of Asia if I had never even discovered it,
and so I killed those people and just said they were
also mutineers from Roldán's crew, so that made
people stop saying that for a while, and for all time
actually, no one else ever said it again, and I might
have to make you sign a non-disclosure agreement
as you read this chapter, as I also made the other
people who I didn't kill that were left, I made them
sign a non-disclosure agreement about me killing
those people and also saying that we did find the
mainland of Asia and that it was not an island
called Cuba, just to be safe, and those agreements
are ironclad, so I think we're good there, and we're
good here with you, the readers, since you signed
the N.D.A.'s, right?

But the thing is, I did start having doubts myself, I
did start to think that it was strange that the people
had not heard of the Grand Kublai Khan or the
Mongols and that they didn't have chopsticks or
sushi or sesame chicken, and they also hadn't heard

of a Great Wall that they had built over many
hundreds of years, you'd think they'd know a little
about that, if it was such a great wall, so either the
wall wasn't that great, which would mean Asia
wasn't that great, or this was a different world, but I
also realized that I did think that the Indians were
liars, and I believed that in my heart I was right,
and my heart is good, it's pure, and very healthy
and I have a strong ticker and will never die, even
though I sometimes feel tired, like right now, and I
also have a strong mind, and so it reasons still that
it was impossible I was wrong.

Many people have said that Columbus started to
lose his mind around the time of this voyage, they
said that the idea that he may have discovered a
New World instead of Asia, made him start to think
that he had actually discovered a third place, not
Asia or a New World, that his mind played a trick
on him, in that it made him start to believe that he
had actually found HEAVEN, and many more
people started to believe that Columbus was
mentally ill, due to his so-called religious delusions
about having found HEAVEN, and though I think I

am definitely a narcissist, and have a narcissistic
personality, there's no doubt about that, but I am
very proud of that, and do not believe it is a bad
thing for me, though maybe it is bad for other
people, but I don't care about other people, and I
never have or will, and I am also very proud of that,
because you can't care what other people think
about you, if you want to be great, you just can't,
that's part of why Roldán was so cool, the not giving
AFs thing that I talked about above, it was funny,
he didn't even give AF when I had him killed for
mutinying my brother, he was very cool about it,
which just made me think he was even cooler than I
did before, ha, classic Roldán, and it just made me
think that a big reason my brother was such a loser,
is that you could see he always cared about other
people and what they thought about the things he
was doing and their effects on other people because
he cared about other people so much, which is what
made him so weak and uncool, both of those things,
but I do want to make it very clear that I am not
anything else in terms of mental problems but a
narcissist, and that I'm a proud narcissist, I have
taken back that stigma, I have taken back the

connotations that narcissism is bad, for me and for other narcissists, and I hope one day, we will just be treated like everyone else who has that mental problem, though I think I will likely be treated better than other narcissists because I'm more special than them, and my narcissism is malignant, which is a special kind of narcissism, and so I am even more special than other people who have a narcissistic personality, because mine is malignant, the most malignant there ever was or ever will be, but the other thing that is more important than that, well, not more important than me having the special kind of malignant narcissism, but it is important, too, because it's something that I did that proves how special my malignant narcissism is, and it is that I did indeed discover HEAVEN, I found it, I did, so yes, besides finding Asia, and a New World, whichever, I also am the first person to get to HEAVEN, and here's how I did that.

...

A Good Cup Of Coffee Is HEAVEN!

One thing that you have to know about HEAVEN is that it is not a place, like Asia or the New World, whichever I found, you have to understand that it is a state, a state in the sense of a state of mind, and you also have to understand that I was the first one to find it, that's the big thing, more than finding that state of mind for yourself, I hope you find out that I found it first, via this book, that you bought, and from there, yes, I do hope you find the state of mind of HEAVEN as well, and that when you are there, you have fun but also pay your respects to me for getting you there, in gold, and so here's how you get there, I'll give you the map to HEAVEN, for free right now, first time is free, OK, it's pretty simple, first you have to get to Asia or the New World, whichever, and then you need to get some cacao beans from the people there, and then you need to brew them into a beverage called coffee, and then drink it, and by God, you will start to feel HEAVEN, I'm talking about the happiness, the energies, the enthusiasm, the state of mind that I call HEAVEN.

The only problem with HEAVEN is that it doesn't
last very long, in fact, no longer than an hour or two
depending on how strong your cacao beans are, and
so the key here is to keep drinking more of the
coffee, because if you stop, then you don't just go
back to the regular world, you crash into a new
state of mind, HELL, which is a really bad
headache, and jitteriness, and heart palpitations,
and lots of peeing, and sometimes the runs, and
most of the time it keeps you up at night, because
you can't sleep from the after-effects, and it's pretty
rough, I'm not going to lie, and sometimes after
some of that HELL, you say, I'm going to give up
this coffee bean, I'm done with it, I got to get off the
bean, HEAVEN isn't worth it, nothing is, but the
next morning, you wake up, and you're usually
pretty tired from not sleeping due to all the
HEAVEN you had too late in the day before, and so
when you wake up you're like, I just gotta get that
bean, dude, I'll feel so much better with some of
that bean, so you just gotta get it, you just gotta do
whatever it takes to get some of that HEAVEN, and
it's so good again after you get it, even better than

you remembered somehow, and I'm on it right now, can't you tell, don't you just feel my happiness and energies, and my state of mind, and isn't it so great and real, that's how I wrote this book, on the bean, in HEAVEN, and you can have it, too, due to me, you can have HEAVEN, HEAVEN, HEAVEN, you don't even need to go to Asia or the New World, like I said before, or even buy this book, though you should buy this book, and so you can get to HEAVEN just by getting some of the coffee, which I've started having shipped over to Europe, for a very good price, it's roasted and artisanal, and it's not fair trade, which some people have complained about, but that's why it's such a good price, the fact that its trade is not fair at all, and no one has complained about its very fair price due to its very unfair trade, I can tell you that, and it's called Columbian Coffee, and it's the best, so go buy some, from the markets where good foods and beverages are sold, and also get some more copies of this book for your friends, because you're going to need it, the HEAVEN, that is, to get through this next part, it was worse than HELL for me.

...

A Witch Hunt!

While I was busy being the first human to find HEAVEN, those so-called religious, righteous sovereigns, Ferdinand and Isabella, were busy showing their true colors, which were very ugly colors, they were hideous colors that were even worse than the paintings of Michelangelo, which are terrible, like I said, I like Raphael!

During the time I was quelling Roldán's rebellion that my tragically uncool and weak brother basically made Roldán do to him, and which made me kill the very cool Roldán for, the sovereigns had started to believe from another rival explorer who pushed his way into their court, who had claimed to have been on my first voyage, though I had never seen or met him, and if I had met him, he wouldn't have left a very good impression because he was a very boring and low-class person, and his name was Amerigo Vespucci, and he said that on the first voyage, I had been very unchristian to the Indians and to my men, and even worse, Amerigo told

Ferdinand and Isabella that he had actually
discovered my lands before me, from the Pinta, or
something, I don't know, his story never really
checked out in the slightest, and he also said that
the lands weren't Asia, that they were definitely a
New World, which he wanted named after himself,
the ego of that man is disgusting, and he wanted
them called the Americas instead of the Amerigos,
for some reason, which just goes to show how dumb
he was, and how he had no sense of marketing or
branding, like me and my Columbian coffee, and
worse than that, Ferdinand and Isabella listened to
him, and they had maps and globes made up that
labeled the land the Americas, and the mainstream
town criers spread this name, too, the liars they are,
and so "America" became the lamestream name for
the land that I found, and it was also just a really
ugly, hideous name, I mean, "America," what kind
of people would want their country called
"America," definitely not a good country of people.

Worse than all that maybe was that Ferdinand and
Isabella sent a judicial investigator to investigate
my behavior, and they sent him all the way to

"America," where I still was, a special counsel, they
called him, and his name was Francisco de
Bobadilla, no relation to Beatriz de Bobadilla,
though he did try to overstep the basis of his
investigation and dig up dirt on me and Beatriz,
and so I called him Bad Bobadilla, and the name
stuck well, because what he did was he led an
absolute witch hunt, this special counsel of his, it
was full of Amerigo's supporters, chock-full of
them, the special counsel was completely biased
against me, and it was very disgraceful because Bad
Bobadilla started to claim I had committed
something he was calling genocide of the Indians,
which didn't seem like a real thing, and worse than
that was he said I was in collusion with a foreign
power to take over Asia or the New World,
whichever, from Ferdinand and Isabella, and to
make a new country of my own, which was very
untrue, again a complete lie made up by Amerigo
and his rigged special counsel, which was an
absolute witch hunt, and a disgrace.

Yes, I wanted to take over the land from Ferdinand
and Isabella, that was true, that was one hundred

percent what I wanted to do, that was my plan all along, the United People of Columbus, a squad goal for me that we've talked about, but I wasn't in collusion with a foreign power to do that, you think I would've wanted another king and queen to rule me, that's just ridiculous, I wanted to be the king myself, and so there was no collusion, absolutely no collusion, no collusion, people!

But to prove that, I would have had to confess to my other crime of plotting to take over the land for myself, and cutting the sovereigns out of the deal, which I wasn't ready to do yet, the cutting out, though I could have done it anytime if I had wanted to, I was ready in many ways, and so I let the special counsel indict me, even though I knew I had done nothing wrong, or at least not the particular thing that the special counsel was set up to investigate me for, and so the special counsel had me board a ship to go back to Spain to see if Ferdinand and Isabella wanted to remove my title of Admiral of the Ocean Sea, which I had won fair and square, also some people thought they could convict me of my crimes, which I guess was

possible, though more people in the judicial system
believed the special counsel's investigation couldn't
lead to criminal charges, just a removal of my title,
and privileges, which were many, in fact, as I was
taken in my boat back to Spain, chained, I should
say, the bastards chained me down in my own hold
for the entire trip, and they didn't even know how
to get back to Spain, so it took many weeks, without
my leadership, months even, maybe even years, it
sure felt like years, down in my own hold, and while
they were mucking about all over the Great Ocean,
using my maps like ball-less cowards, I wrote down
all the privileges I wanted back from Bad Bobadilla,
who had seized them from me, in the name of the
King and Queen, and I wrote a Book of Privileges to
make sure I got them back, and it was a much
longer book than this one, I wish I had it still,
though, if I have time to remember all the privileges
I might put it all in here as an appendix to this
book, we'll see, we'll see if there's enough time
before I die, but there likely will be, because I am
not tired right now, not at all, though I am fairly
tired, probably more tired than most people could
handle, but not me, I can handle how tired I am, as

I must continue to tell you about how the witch
hunt special counsel, Bad Bobadilla, he stole it from
me, when he found it, my Book of Privileges, and
made fun of the fact that I kept a Book of Privileges,
and made fun of me very cruelly.

And that's what happens when there's a witch hunt,
bad stuff happens to a good leader who has done so
many good things for his people it's crazy, it's crazy
that you could remove someone, who has done so
many good things, from power for abusing his
power, that that happened to me, that is just nuts,
and many times I just chose not to acknowledge it
even happened to me, and I probably wouldn't have
talked about it now, if not for the fact that the other
thing that happens during a witch hunt is that the
people who do the witch-hunting get their
comeuppance as well, you'll see, the people who
witch-hunted me, they got their comeuppance very
badly, from me, because I was too great for them.

...

My Second Term, That's Right I Won A Second Term!

Though I had initially been stripped of my title of
Admiral of the Ocean Sea and its privileges due to
the special counsel, Bad Bobadilla, that is to also
say, I was impeached from my term as Admiral of
the Ocean Sea, what happened next was that, the
people, they told Ferdinand and Isabella if you
don't reinstate Columbus, we will riot in the streets,
and they were going to do it, they were really going
to do it, that's how much they columbused me,
many of the people, and it was a scary thing for
some of the people who were kind of sick of me, but
it was also a great thing for me, because more of the
people were going to really riot in the streets unless
I was reinstated, it wasn't just something I kept
saying over and over again in cryptic but also very
explicit ways that probably wouldn't actually
happen, it would have happened, but so what
happened was Columbus did get a second term as
Admiral of the Ocean Sea, and it was a great thing,
for I was even more unstoppable this time, and so I

had Bad Bobadilla, the special counsel, dismissed,
and he was no longer a threat to me, nor was
anyone, and I knew that, in all likelihood, I could be
Admiral of the Ocean Sea for my entire life, if I
really forced the issue, if I didn't give in, if I fought
tooth and nail, claw and paw, is that a phrase, it
should be, I'm going to make it one, claw and paw,
and if I never gave up, no matter the consequences
to anyone else besides myself, and if I didn't care
what happened to other people in the world due to
my ambition, I realized I could achieve anything,
and it was the greatest realization of my life, and
one of the greatest realizations in any life in history,
that there was no limit to what Columbus could do
for himself, and I was very happy.

However, I then realized that even though I had
made sure that my sons would eventually take over
my title again, I saw how unfair the world could be,
in that, really great people like me, the best person
to ever live, he can lose power as fast as he got it,
and that the people on top, there is actually only a
thin veneer between their rise and their fall, and
that was kind of scary, because I always assumed

once I had my title that I was unimpeachable and
that my privileges were forever untouchable, so that
new realization that that might not always be the
case made me very scared, and I thought that if I
died, maybe my sons wouldn't know that they just
needed to never give up their ambition to keep
power, or that they wouldn't know enough about
Asia slash the New World, whichever it turned out
to be, to rule it properly, with their title, and so I
resolved that with my second term I would work
toward cementing my legacy so that my offspring
could rule after me forever, but I was sad that I
didn't have a daughter to rule after me, and I would
have favored her over my sons, who were a little
dumb and they sort of, like, never grew up beyond
being man-children, to be honest, and made many
careless mistakes, particularly in regards to the
special counsel, as Diego, my older son, actually did
take some meetings with foreign powers, which
made no sense because I told him we were just
going to become the kings of the land ourselves, we
didn't need to collude with foreign powers, you
idiot apple of mine, and I don't know, something
must have got mucked up in between that idiot

apple of mine's ears and his brain, and so that created some real problems for me in terms of the witch hunt, and, thinking about it more now, if I had had the daughter I always wanted, I would have positioned her as a softer power so that she would be more agreeable to the people of the new land that would have been ours, but I didn't have her, and so she didn't become the first female explorer, and so I was stuck with my sons, and so I didn't trust Diego anymore after the fact that he colluded behind my back on my behalf, when I didn't want any collusion, I had said no collusion, no collusion, that was not a thing that I wanted, or did myself, but he had colluded, and so he was dead to me, like my brother, and my first wife, and Felicia, bye, Felicia, so I brought my younger son, Ferdinand, with me for my final voyage.

Or the final voyage as of right now, because that could still change, I haven't decided if it's final yet, that voyage, and I'm not sure when I will fully decide that, we'll see, you never know with me, that's what makes me so exciting, though, and so great, besides always saying that I am great, the

123

other thing that is so great about me is the
cliffhangers, isn't it, are you enjoying the
cliffhangers in this book, it's like my life is one long
dramatic play, I wish people could watch it unfold
on, like, a small screen or something, in their
homes, and be very comfortable, even if the events
themselves that they witness are very
uncomfortable, the drama of my life, it unfolds in
front of their eyes, with my amazing exploits,
maybe I will invent such a technology, some screens
that people watch all the time, before I go on
another final voyage, or maybe I won't, but you're
excited about it, I can see, see, I did it again, I got
you excited for something I said I might do, OK, but
first, here's something that I already did, which is a
big deal, perhaps bigger than anything I could think
of cliffhangering you all with, though, we'll see,
maybe there is something bigger that I could say as
a cliffhanger, you never know, actually, yeah,
another thing that I also want to do before dying,
besides those first screens, is other screens that I
could put my words onto at any time, so that
everyone all over the world could just see whatever
I want them to see just by me writing words onto

my screen, that would be a very powerful thing and
a great thing that I think I will do, for sure, yes, I
will do that, and it will be great, and I will call it a
trumpet, for though it will not literally be a musical
instrument, it will be an instrument by which I will
trumpet my great words across the whole world,
which will be a great thing for the world, though I
am getting very tired, and I fear I am near the end
of this tale, or at least the telling of this tale, and I
wonder maybe if I finish telling this tale, will my life
end, if I stop speaking all the time, non-stop,
running my mouth, will I extinguish, and how very
sad that would be to finish my tale, and my life, and
for the trumpet to go quiet, and be gone from this
world forever, how very sad indeed, but it will never
happen, I am sure of it, though I am very tired, it is
true that I am tired, more tired than I have ever
been, but that's OK, I'm OK, because the trumpet
that I will invent will keep my words alive forever as
well as this book which I will publish on it, or
maybe on the first screens, I'm not sure, it's all very
confusing what I am imagining, it feels so real, but
so impossible, but also very likely to happen, it is
very dream-like but a little nightmarish potentially,

too, and I am very tired, it's possible no one has
ever been so tired as me right now or ever will be,
and I am even tiring of saying that phrase, the
phrase now or ever will be, and I am maybe most
tired of being me, it is very tiring being me, people
don't realize that, it is my cross to bear, I guess,
being me, how hard that is, how tiring I am, even to
myself, but I will finish the chapter and the book,
for I am me, I am Columbus.

I should also say that when Ferdinand and Isabella
reinstated my title, they did so in name only, as
Isabella died, and Ferdinand turned out to be an
Indian giver, on the privileges side of the deal, it's
sad but true, that was the only bad deal I ever
struck, and even if I don't want it to be true, I guess
I could lie and say it wasn't the truth, but I think as
I get tired I am losing my desire to control your
perception of me, which is probably a mistake, I
may have made some mistakes in my life, not many,
but there may have probably been a lot, actually I
am sure of it, I have made some very bad mistakes
that have hurt many many many people, maybe,
and if so, I am sorry for them, in fact, I am very

sorry, and I have not apologized to anyone before, and I thought I never would, but it is nice to do it here now, it feels like a great weight has been lifted from me, but probably not from the people I have hurt, so I take it back, because apologies are pointless, I take it back, if it's with my last dying breath, I take it back, my apology, as well as any apologies I might ever make, do you hear that, I am so tired, I hope it is not my last breath this one, the one with which I am taking back any and all apologies, I hope it is not my last breath that extinguishes the trumpet, but I am so very tired.

...

The Final Voyage And How I Met Anacabo And Also How I Saved All The People Of Earth From These Beings From The Sky, It's A Big Chapter In My Life And In The Book And It Should Be In The History Books, Too, For Sure, So Read To The End!

It is true I am getting very tired, I have done a lot with my life, including writing this great history book about me, and it has taken a lot out of me, but I will rally my formidable energies and spare no fiber of my being to share what happened on the final voyage with my son, Ferdinand, and how I met Anacabo, who is here with me still, dutifully writing this all down, as my slave and friend and lover, and I'm sure, even though I can no longer see her, because I am blind, due to what happened on the final voyage, but I am sure that she's here, and I'm sure that she is writing these words down, and that these words will be read one day, because I believe in my reality and that it is more real than anyone else's, and so what I am about to tell you has never

been told to anyone, and if it is not shared by
Anacabo, it will be lost to history, which would not
only be very sad for me, but it would also be very
sad for you, if you can't read this, though I am sure
you are reading this, and I guess I am really feeling
the seasickness of Columbus' words right now, it is
very hard to continue speaking, the wild seesawing
has taken a great toll on me, speaking my words has
been very hard for me, the syntax, up down, up
down, and all about, back forth, back forth, to the
starboard and the port sides of the words, so
erratic, without any coherency, and in apparent
insanity, and I'm sure the repetitive diction is also
very bad, it's bad, very bad, and it must signify
some sort of great cognitive decline, that must be
so, and it must be so tiring for you, too, dear reader,
but bear with me, for I must finish, for I fear the
end is near, and so I must tell you what happened.

My son and I, we sailed back to Asia slash the New
World, it really doesn't matter which of those it
was, it really doesn't matter, I'm tired of that
argument, it is very tiresome to me, that ceaseless
argument, and I am very tired, do you not hear me,

when I tell you that I am tired of talking about that,
and that I am very tired, do you not hear me!

Do not make me talk about that anymore, I have
more important things to share now, and what that
is, is what was it, damnit, I am so, it was that what
we found when we went back there, ahh, I am
getting so tired, I can barely bear it, what it was,
was that I was trying to, I can't remember what I
said earlier, did I tell you before, chapters back, that
the people when we landed, they said we were
"beings from the sky," did I say that, I may not have
said that, but it is what happened, they believed we
were beings from the sky, an alien species, and I
thought it was a very dumb thing to say, frankly,
but I guess also understandable, because I am so
unique, and so special, and so it did make some
sense, because I was basically a different species
than all of them, because I am so special, but it
made a lot more sense on the final voyage, when we
got back there, and we got shipwrecked and
stranded on an island, and it was a bad situation, it
was very bad, and it didn't look good, and there was
a chance, a real chance, that my son and I would die

there, on that cursed shipwrecked island, that we

would vanish from the world, and from history

potentially, but the Indians they were very nice to

us, and they brought us food and they dressed our

wounds, and it was weird because we had always

been more powerful than them, and they had

always been at our mercy, but this time, I was at

their mercy, for we were so weak, even weaker than

I am right now, and they could have slaughtered us

all if they wanted to, and I realized then that

sometimes the meek are not meeker than the

strong, even though they are the meek and I am the

strong, and always have been and will be, and I am

so tired right now, of saying that, and of being me,

but I must say that I realized then that under

different circumstances different things could have

happened in history, and I wondered if maybe I had

come to the New World slash Asia, it doesn't

matter, at a different time, perhaps a few hundred

years earlier, there may have been another

civilization there, for some reason, the name

"Mayans" came to my mind, and I wondered what

would happen if our civilization collided with a

hypothetical civilization called the Mayans, when

they were at their peak, like we were at ours when
we came to Asia slash the New World, I'm tired of,
I'm so very tired, but I think we still would have
been the winners, because we win, win, man, I am
so tired, so very tired of being me, but what I must
say is, I was thinking then it just goes to show when
two worlds collide there is much conflict and it can
lead to the loss of a people and a culture and that
that could have been us, maybe.

And suddenly I thought of an even bigger thing, as I
was weak and shipwrecked, and more tired than I
am now, which is the most tired I have ever been,
so maybe I am more meek now than then, and
maybe I am meek as well as strong sometimes, I do
not know, what I'm saying is that I thought then,
what if another species, a non-human species, what
if it came not from somewhere on Earth, not a
proverbial New World, but an actual New World, I
thought what if this species came from another
planet, and they landed on Earth, would they be
stronger than us humans, even if all of us realized
that we were one people finally, and fought together
for the first time as one, and there was no more

petty tribalism, just one race, and would we win, or
would these aliens overrun us, like I had overrun
the Indians, and how Dad and me had been overrun
by the Adornos, and how the Indians could have
overrun me and my son while shipwrecked and at
their mercy, and I grew very scared, but then I
thought that me and the humans would definitely
win, and that I would survive this shipwreck and be
rescued with my son, like Dad and me had survived
the Adornos, and I would live on to write a great
book about it, because I was destined for greatness,
and so is humanity, and nothing can stop us,
because all we do is, you know what we do, I don't
have to say it, I'm so tired, I'm so very tired, of
being me, but I must tell you what happened next, I
must, and I will, for I am me, I am Columbus.

Because just then, from the sky, came a being, a
very beautiful green being, with skin that was
somehow even more beautiful than my white skin,
but the skin, though, it changed color to other
colors, it was a mixture of all colors, it went to black
and then to white, like mine, and brown, like the
natives, which I realize was as beautiful as my skin

then, and back to green and it was all colors and none at all, and then this being was a female and then a male and then neither and both and something else, and all of them were equally good, and it declared that its name was Anacabo, and even though she wishes that I refer to her as a they, I still call her a her, call me old-fashioned, and she calls me her Don, or her Don Quixote, and she is a being from the sky, an alien, and she, sorry, they, I'll say they from now on, I promise, because I love they, and they taught me so much, and so I will share what I learned from them, the aliens, for Anacabo is not just Anacabo, Anacabo is all of their species at all times, and each of them are all of the others, at the same times, too, for they are one species, one kind, and they are all they, for all time, and the learning of that was more important than anything I had ever done, and that is what is finally humbling me now, I can feel a great humbling now, and I am humbled now, I am humbled.

As I lay here, on my deathbed, as I lay dying, for they have humbled me, they have humbled they, it is so nice, thank you, they, it is humbling to realize

they were also they, the beings from the sky, the
Indians and the Europeans and Amerigo and the
special counsel and the sovereigns and my sons and
the Indian that was coughed on that was loved, and
Filipa, and Father, and Brother, and the Indians,
were the Indians said yet, they should be called the
Taínos, and Anacabo, and Columbus, they are all
they, and as they lie down to die someday, which is
all days, they will look down on who they were, as
part of a continuum of one they, that has hurt and
helped the same they, and they will know this now,
at their death, as they die, as they die, right now.

As well as here, at the end of this book, of which
hopefully a good time reading was had, or, if
skipped to the end, a good time reading will be had,
and the learning to live together was or will be
done, and that a celebration of that with a holiday
was or will be started, and maybe it also was or will
be a paid holiday used to elect new leaders, and its
name was or will be decided, by they, bye, they.

...

..

.

FAKE HISTORY! The Story Of How Fake Historians Treated Christopher Columbus Very Very Unfairly

This is a work of parody and satire. Any similarity to or mention of real people, places, or events is meant to function as parody and satire.

Made in the USA
Monee, IL
23 May 2020